Consumption and its Consequences

Consumption and its Consequences

Daniel Miller

polity

First published in 2012 by Polity Press

Polity Press
65 Bridge Street
Cambridge CB2 1UR, UK

Polity Press
350 Main Street
Malden, MA 02148, USA

ISBN-13: 978-0-7456-6107-0
ISBN-13: 978-0-7456-6108-7 (pb)

A catalogue record for this book is available from the British Library.

Typeset in 11 on 13 pt Sabon
by Toppan Best-set Premedia Limited
Printed and bound in Great Britain by MPG Books Group Limited

For further information on Polity, visit our website: www.politybooks.com

Contents

Prologue

This book is the sequel to the volume *Stuff*.[1] While *Stuff* sum-marised my previous writings on material culture, this companion volume summarises my research on consumption, but then pro-ceeds to discuss the consequences of consumption. The core of the book is addressed to the question of what consumption is and why we consume. But three of the chapters look more to the consequences of consumption, with particular reference to rethink-ing the nature of political economy and questioning current pro-posals for achieving environmental sustainability. Many of the issues of politics and economics that were absent from *Stuff* are central here. It follows that this is a much more opinionated book, where I feel it is important to take a stance on a wide variety of current concerns.

The problem is that this requires a rather different kind of volume from one that summarises the outcome of research. I don't have just one simple stance on what are mainly highly complex issues. I can see the merits in a variety of equally powerful and persuasive positions, and trying to wish away that diversity of argument and pretend to stand for only one position would be false. For this reason I have written the first and final chapters of this book, those which are most replete with opinions and political comment, as a dialogue between three fictional characters called Mike, Chris and Grace. Each of them represents a different version of my views which remain in argument with each other. As you shall soon discover, Mike represents a largely green perspective, Chris represents a mainly red perspective, while Grace represents the many years I have spent as an anthropological fieldworker living with people in poverty. I am not quite sure what it says about me, that two aspects of my own personality appear here as married to each other, but let's not go there.

But, having adopted this ruse, I think in compensation I should also say a few words about what I see as the core of my political and academic grounding. I am a qualitative fieldworker who relies on interpretation and harbours a suspicion of quantitative and experimental research when applied to human and social behaviour. I see most pseudo-scientific work within psychology, economics and sociology as highly problematic because the data is often removed from its original context, simplified and distorted in order to fit within quantification and experiment. I appreciate that these same *scientists* may in turn consider my own work to be entirely without merit, since from their stance my data do not equate to scientific proof. On the other hand, I am no post-modern relativist when it comes to knowledge. Anthropology depends on the hard slog of at least a year's fieldwork, patiently accumulating information. I wouldn't bother doing this if I didn't intend that all my work should correspond to what could be called evidence-based scholarship. But I have found that trying to prove something is usually what prevents us from managing to understand something. There is more extensive discussion of these epistemological issues within this book.

I was educated into politics mainly through discussions of Marxism. But forget the image of revolutionary cabals in smoke-filled rooms. One of the three A-level textbooks in politics assigned by my – anything but revolutionary – school was *The Communist Manifesto*. I then became interested in the background to these writings, and today I would regard the philosopher Hegel along with the anthropologists Lévi-Strauss and Bourdieu as my three principal academic mentors. I also came to see many problems with the variety of socialist ideals in which I initially believed as a student. The first was that pure critique was almost inevitably self-indulgent and regressive. The second was that this was equally true of the advocacy of utopian alternatives to the status quo. Instead, I have come to believe that the best way of insisting that some things in the modern world are not only thoroughly unjust

but also unacceptable is by pointing out that there already exist
entirely feasible alternatives which, while not perfect, are demon-
strably better.

So when I teach about consumption I always start by asking
students to think of their prime example of a consumer society as
not the US but Norway – for the simple reason that, when it comes
to politics over the last few decades, I just can't think of a prefer-
able example that actually exists. Norway is just as wealthy and
capitalist as the UK or the US. Yet it has become and remains one
of the wealthiest countries today, in combination with perhaps the
strongest commitment to social egalitarianism and social welfare
anywhere in the world. Its political intelligence in storing the
legacy of its oil wealth, rather than squandering it in political
advantage, leaves me close to awestruck. It defies textbook economics, since it shows how a society can be hugely successful in
wealth creation while having comparatively limited investment in
either individualism or competition. If the rest of the world could
come closer to Norway, it would not be utopia, but we would be
hugely improved. And my point is that Norway already exists. So,
in reading this book, you can assume that I aspire to a variant of
social democracy looking for the best and most pragmatic combination of the following: much more tightly regulated capitalist
commerce, an egalitarian and humanistic social welfare system,
and an ethical concern for the future of the planet and a sustainable environment. I have no problem repeating the cliché that I
have children and a concern with the legacy the present bequeaths
to the future. Finally, I am an inveterate optimist. I will argue in
this book that the world has consistently improved in terms of the
welfare of most of its populations and there are good reasons for
thinking it will continue to do so. I assume this last may be a
thoroughly unpopular and irritating stance.

I should also point out that the core of this book is very different from the frame that surrounds it. The device of the first and
last chapters is intended to deal with the diversity of political and
other opinions that are commonly expressed regarding the consequences of consumption, the problems it causes and the proffered
solutions. But the middle chapters are there for quite another
purpose. They comprise a summary of research I have been
engaged in for over two decades. One of my principal ambitions
has been to rescue the study of consumption from being reduced

to such matters of moral adjudication or political stance. These chapters are much more to do with trying to provide a scholarly foundation to what I think most consumption actually is rather than what we would like to project upon it. The core concern is with everyday household provisioning. I want to bring this back to the level of buying toilet rolls and cans of soup or replacing worn blue jeans – also to being able to possess a car, a computer and a mobile phone, which seems foundational to our new, but quickly taken for granted, capacities in the world. This book addresses directly the consequences of consumption such as the impact on climate change and in legitimating the political economy. But consequences are not necessarily causes. When it comes to understanding why people consume, I will focus much more on how goods work within our core relationships to the people with whom we live and most care about. There is a chapter that is concerned primarily with how shopping is used as a technology for the expression and establishment of love within households. One of the main reasons we may consume a huge range of quite similar goods such as clothes and food is that these become a kind of vocabulary that allow us richly to express these core relationships – for example, with our children. If you consider the hundreds of pages a novelist might expend in describing a single relationship, it is not surprising that we feel that there cannot ever be enough variety of goods actually to reach the level of nuance to which we would aspire in our engagement with another person we care about – or indeed with ourselves.

A further chapter is concerned more with how cosmological ideas to do with time are expressed through the order of things, ranging from car upholstery to the celebration of Christmas. I will explore local symbolic systems based on the divisions of ethnicity, class and gender. The focus is not, however, on difference, not even on status differences or emulation, which have dominated past theories of consumption. In fact, my discussion ends with a chapter on why and how people struggle to become merely ordinary. This is why I prefer to separate out these middle chapters, with their ethnographic research and conclusions as to what consumption actually is, from the opinions and debates about its consequences.

I will not repeat the extensive two pages of acknowledgments provided in *Stuff*, since they pertain to both books equally. They include all the PhD students I have supervised, my work colleagues in the Department of Anthropology at University College London, and especially my co-researchers on various past projects, most of which have been conducted in collaboration with others, as well as the very considerable number of people who have been generous with their time and information as informants on these projects.

To the names listed in *Stuff* I would add those whom I have come to know since. In the last two years I have gained some new colleagues in material culture studies: Lane DeNicola and Ludovic Coupeye, as well as Rebecca Empson in social anthropology; some new PhD students, Nick Gadsby and Tiziana Traldi; and the students in our new degree course of digital anthropology. Julie Botticello has been of particular help in day-to-day matters. Finally, there are those people who have made comments or helped edit this particular manuscript: the anonymous readers found by my publisher, Rebecca Empson, Turo-Kimmo Lehtonen, Tom McDonald, Roxana Morosco, Razvan Nicolescu, John Thompson, Hal Wilhite, Richard Wilk and, especially, Cynthia Isenhour and Tania Lewis. Special thanks to Rickie Burman for her support and considerable help in copy-editing.

1

What's Wrong with Consumption?

The scene

The conversation takes place in the kitchen of Mike's comfortable North London home.

Mike is in his late fifties. You can see his hair was once chestnut, though now what's left is mainly grey. A quick glance at the labels of organic and other products on the shelves tells you he sits clearly in the green corner, but also that he is something of a hobbyist with respect to technologies and gadgets. He is a professor of environmental studies.

Chris is in his mid-forties, not well favoured in looks, but possessing a face that makes him appear quick and lively, always ready to argue and expecting to win. Within a few sentences it is clear that he sits firmly in the red corner. He is a senior lecturer in sociology.

Grace is in her late thirties – slim, with long hair, and attractive. Born in the Philippines, she is married to Chris. She is a lecturer in anthropology. She smiles a lot, sometimes wryly, especially when Chris is talking.

Mike met Chris and Grace recently at a conference on consumption and the environment. When he realised that all three teach courses about consumption within their respective disciplines, he decided to invite them over for what he hoped would be the first of many discussions. Being professional academics, they agreed that they would each come ready to discuss some books, ideally something classic they use in teaching and also something new, that would illustrate their respective approaches to consumption. This first meeting takes place at Mike's house.

MIKE: That is so purple, it's beyond purple. Are you really telling me there is no artificial colour in it? But it's also delicious. What did you say it's called?

GRACE: Ube, and, given that I made it with my own fair hands, I think I can vouch for the contents. Ube is simply our word for purple yam, but for this dessert, which is one of the most common in the Philippines, you add condensed milk, butter and sugar. Some people also add coconut milk. Glad you like it. When a friend of mine, who lives in Manila, has visitors from abroad she always takes them first to one of our fast food outlets, where the most common dessert is ice cream made with ube topped by grated cheese. It certainly satisfies their desire for the exotic.

MIKE: OK, well, I think I'd better start our conversation, if only to stop myself devouring the lot. So, when we met I recall we hoped for three initial meetings: today's would be generally about consumption, the second devoted to practical solutions to problems arising from consumption and climate change, and the third a comparison of our course contents for our teaching on consumption. So perhaps we should start off by outlining our positions on consumption. I should be upfront and confess that I simply can't help but feel that those of us in environmental studies occupy a kind of higher ground in the arguments about consumption. The simple point is that you can discuss all you like about the causes, the meaning and the nature of consumption, and obviously I work on these issues. But today you have to see this primarily as a contribution to an imperative which cuts straight through all such debates, and it emanates from the green position to which I have devoted my academic life.

Actually, more than my academic life. I was only a teenager in 1972 when I first heard about something called *The Limits to Growth* that had been issued by an organisation called the Club of Rome.[1] I was quite proud of the fact that I managed to get hold of a copy. It was really the first time the general public had any indication at all of what was to become the core of the green movement. It set out the proposition that our planet's resources are finite and irreplaceable. Of course, at that time, whenever I tried to convince my family and friends that this was a kind of global wake-up call, they dismissed me like I was some kind of freak. I suppose my purple flared trousers and flowered shirts didn't help.

GRACE: Sorry, I just need a second to get myself into the flower shirt image. Do you have any photographs? Hair length?

MIKE: That's why you really don't want to see the photos. My hair just didn't suit long. It just gave me that drugged up and dozy look. Have you read Linda Grant's new novel, *We Had it So Good*?[2] It took me back to those days. Anyway, being an incipient green at that time was taken simply as further sign of my stupidity, not my prescience; they thought I was on another planet rather than trying to save this one.

The blessing of hair loss is that I now seem to be taken quite seriously. It's amazing how things have gone into reverse. When we are told Republican politicians in the US don't believe in climate change, we see this as a sign that they are either buffoons or liars.

CHRIS: Why do you think that is?

MIKE: Well partly, I guess, this reflects the shift away from the main point made in *The Limits to Growth* about natural resources. That was a complex position because the consideration of each resource led to a specific argument as to how much of it actually exists. It probably hasn't helped that estimates for oil and other natural elements kept being under-estimated, and soon we sounded like we were crying wolf. Again, we have problems when people realise that what we call rare earths include some sub-stances that are not at all rare. Today we tend to have a single focus upon climate change, which makes it rather simpler to put the case for being green. It is much easier to focus upon the over-whelming evidence for this one trajectory, with potentially even more catastrophic consequences than the depletion of each particular resource.

GRACE: So you're saying that it's just easier and simpler to convince people about one thing, which is global warming.

MIKE: Precisely. As it happens, the fourth report of the IPCC in 2007 and the Stern Report[3] of around the same time brought the economists out firmly on our side, and my sense is that, once you have the econo-mists, you find that both the politicians and the media these days tend to follow slavishly whatever they say. As a result, at least in the UK, it feels like the issue of evidence has been largely won.

GRACE: So what are the implications for our discussion of consumption?

MIKE: Well, for me, the question 'What is consumption?' is no longer just some rarefied academic debate of only esoteric or commercial interest. It becomes the single most pressing point of academic enquiry, since we urgently need to commit unequivocally to an immediate and sustained reduction in con-sumption. We are at a particularly dangerous moment when the vast populations of China and South Asia seem poised to launch an assault intended to reach our levels of consumption in the shortest possible time. Given that they represent the major-ity of the world's population, and that even current levels of consumption are unsustainable, this will be environmentally catastrophic. It means that our children and grandchildren will inherit less of a planet – or at least less of its landmass – and face vast changes in agriculture to which they may find it impossible to adapt. So we can't duck this one. If we gather here today to talk about consumption, it is surely with the essential aim of reducing it.

OK so this explains the two books I have brought for discussion today. One is called *Why We Disagree about Climate Change*, by Mike Hulme, and the other is *Heat*, by George Monbiot.[4] You may find the first an odd choice, since it makes almost no mention of consumption. So let me start with the more straightforward position, which is that of Monbiot.

GRACE: Oh, I am a huge fan of Monbiot. I read *The Guardian* daily and I always reckon that Jonathan Freedland helps me understand the reasons why I think what I think, Monbiot gives me the critical ammunition that other journalists won't, and I practically stalk Hadley Freeman.

MIKE: Hadley Freeman?

CHRIS: She writes mainly on fashion, but hilarious. She also helps men avoid inadvertent crimes, like double denim.

MIKE: Well, I am sticking with Monbiot for now – he deals with crimes of a slightly larger scale than double denim. What I love about his work is the sheer relentlessness. His style of argument creates a clear road from knowledge to necessary action as an absolute logic of common sense – a sort of 'given that, we must surely do this' style. And there are always twists in the tail of consequence. So we might just think we need to reduce energy use in the home. But then he predicts that those energy savings will actually lead to greater energy expenditure, as we will put any time and money gained into some other energy-inefficient activity. So each trajectory of effects has to be followed through until there is a demonstrable payoff in the overall saving of energy, a plausible solution that will work. He also shares my love of sorting such plausible science from science fiction. One of my friends constantly derides the way I keep coming up with what he calls my 'small boy dreams big idea that saves the planet' stuff, which he blames on my reading too many Superman comics as a kid.

CHRIS: You mean that poster on the wall is your doing, not your kids'?

MIKE: Absolutely. Anyway, in 2006 Monbiot was talking about turning cement, whose production at that time created more carbon dioxide, into a new kind of cement that would absorb carbon dioxide. Now, in 2011, this is starting to look like a serious possibility with companies such as Novacem. In fact he is very useful for our discussion of consumption because a lot of his concerns relate to home and transport in these – pun alert – very concrete ways.

CHRIS: Oh, good, puns are allowed then!

MIKE: Of course. Monbiot is also great at exposing the hypocrisies common among all of us who want to appear visibly green, such as flying across the world for eco-holidays which create unnecessary carbon miles.

GRACE: Oh, and of course we had to go there because we were due to give a paper at an academic conference, and the one in Vietnam was so much more relevant than the one in Loughborough. And, once you were there, the fact that there was a resort nearby...

CHRIS: Before you go on, Mike, to be honest, we have both read Monbiot, but not this other one, Mike Hulme?

MIKE: Oh, OK. Well, I rather like the juxtaposition of Monbiot and Hulme, which is a bit of a 'ships passing in the night' comparison. Monbiot, as I understand it, was not trained in science, but his book is in thrall to science and replete with statistics. By contrast, Hulme reads like a scientist on a journey to somewhere else. He's actually one of the leading figures in the science of climate change, but recently he has steered his course to a land of radical doubt, against the presumption of some pure science decontextualised from cultural life.

CHRIS: Are we talking Bruno Latour?[5]

MIKE: Yes, that would be fair. Hulme notes that climate change involves a complex set of variables only some of which could ever be subject to the kind of testable quantitative analysis that we imagine as science. But his point is that most climate scientists are perfectly sensible to a situation where they can provide estimates of risk only within wide parameters. They have just as much a problem with media that think, because they are called scientists, they must be purveyors of certainty through clear, repeatable, testable and definitive results.

GRACE: The waves will start lapping at Buckingham Palace on the first of June 2023.

MIKE: That sort of thing. Hulme then suggests that the results of climate science are better regarded as a kind of discourse that we only ever see through the lens of some or other interested group. Economists turn it into measures of value and create a carbon market to trade with. Activists turn it into a condemnation of the capitalist system and grounds for revolution. Governments turn it into a security risk to be treated as a global threat on a par with terrorism. Everyone sees it in their own light because, in the end, it is a form of risk, and people assess risks differently.

            To add further complexity, the problem of climate change is always relative to people's particular situation. It's an urgent priority for people who live on low-lying Pacific atolls, less for an inland nation protected from sea-level rises. It may conflict with another priority such as poverty reduction.

CHRIS: Too right. Biofuels may look attractive from a green perspective but take vast amounts of land from food production and thereby decrease food security. There are things your lot are doing which clearly increase poverty.

MIKE: Acknowledged. And Hulme sees this clearly. His aim is not ultimately to weaken the green case. He clearly feels that, actually to have the requisite impact, climate science needs to work with this plurality and messiness rather than wish it away. So that's really why I brought both books. I always start by giving Monbiot to the students. He works brilliantly for the kind of shock and awe impact that helps create green activists. But I am a bit long in the tooth, and since *The Limits to Growth* I have seen both the statistics and the main green arguments change again and again. So I like to temper Monbiot with Hulme, and cook up a dish of science flavoured with doubt.

GRACE: That's quite funny, because that exactly describes your response to my ube; you ate it, but it was like you couldn't quite believe it.

CHRIS (laughs): OK, but it's a pretty hard dish to reject.

MIKE: I am not quite sure if you're referring to ube or to my metaphorical dish. But I guess it's true of both. OK then, Chris, since you see yourself as the more political animal, let me move things in that direction a bit. For me, the climate change clouds have a silver lining. They give us the ammunition to deal with those desperate problems of modern life, materialism and over-consumption.

I speak from the heart because I can't help thinking, maybe obsessing, about my own sixteen-year-old son. He only ever seems interested in the most mindless materialism – a life devoted to computer games, hair styles created with some revolting gel, the latest smart phone. His only aspirations are towards whatever job might make him so rich that he can immediately gratify every whim, from the jacuzzi in the garden to the flashy car. He has become devoted to unbelievably expensive male perfumes that only suggest to me how gullible he has become, and undermine the basic respect I would like to have in my own son.

I don't want to pre-empt your stance, Chris, but I suspect that, like me, you believe that under a market system we can never say that the success of a product is evidence that it serves the welfare of consumers. We can only assume it has thereby served the profits of commerce.

CHRIS: I think I can live with that characterisation, though I'm not sure I always want to be seen as so predictable.

MIKE: I don't know anything about that fashion reporter you seem to follow, but it seems to me we are flooded with the most ridiculous amounts of new fashions which serve only the makers of walk-in wardrobes. And to be able to afford all this consumption we create an ever more heartless system of employment that in turn results in unprecedented levels of stress and overwork. The green connection is partly that I think we fail to prevent the imminent destruction of the planet partly because we are losing our ability to appreciate nature. And partly because I think we can kill these two vultures that plague our world with the same stone. I am not a religious man, but I have to believe there is something transcendent in life itself that we see in nature. I go hiking at weekends just to find places some distance from this deluge of commodities. There I breathe in more than fresh air. I regain some sort of connection with nature, an appreciation of bird sound and the profusion of wild flowers, of landscapes and seabirds soaring above cliffs.

So, whatever the difference between Monbiot and Hulme, all green thinking involves a much bigger system of basic values and ethics. We can't but regard the environmental crisis as also something of a saviour, a means to resurrect some form of morality, to rethink basic human values. It's a once-only opportunity to retract this ugly and facile consumerism and actually end up with not just a happier planet but a happier population. I guess you have also read Layard's book *Happiness*[6] and the Easterlin Paradox.

CHRIS: I have read Layard, but the other thing? Sounds like science fiction.

MIKE: I suppose it does a bit. Actually it comes from a
              1970s paper[7] by the economist Richard Easterlin,
              who was the first to demonstrate that, in compar-
              ing countries (though not within countries), there
              was no clear statistical association between higher
              incomes and levels of reported happiness. He paved
              the way for Layard and the other economists who
              are trying to make happiness the measure of eco-
              nomic success rather than simply income.[8] I think
              this just confirms what we already know from our
              own experience about wealth not bringing happi-
              ness. So let me conclude my 'where I am coming
              from' bit. I am essentially interested in understand-
              ing consumption in order to create an effective
              means of curbing excessive consumption – firstly for
              the sake of the planet but also for the sake of our
              souls.

GRACE: Thanks for that, Mike. Well, we needn't have
              worried about whether we would find ourselves a
              good argument, because, as the saying is, I couldn't
              agree with you less. But if you ended on a personal
              note, to explain your stance, perhaps I should start
              on one. I want to tell you something of my history.
              One hears about Asian tigers, but the Philippines, I
              am afraid, is an Asian sloth.[9] Nothing we have tried
              to do to get our economy moving seems to have
              worked. The rest of South-East Asia leaps ahead
              and we are left behind. Most families traditionally
              worked, as mine did, as tenant farmers. This meant
              we had to be able to afford to rent the very land we
              farmed. One year my parents invested in a new
              crop, a kind of maize that had a sweeter taste. But
              the trouble was that everyone in our area had the
              same idea, and the price collapsed. So the next year
              my family didn't even have the money to rent land
              and couldn't farm. But they had started to invest in
              me. I had managed to win pretty much every schol-
              arship to better education open to me. Being in state
              schools, I started with very limited prospects, but I
              was seen as a swot and a star. I loved school. In

such cases most kids learn nursing, but even with those scholarships the cost of such training was beyond our means. So I got as far as nursing assist-ant. My family couldn't afford the next step, which was to send me abroad, but, as is often the case, the more extended family joined in. One uncle even sold some land. Twice we gave money to agencies who kept it and turned out to be running scams. Even more family members had to be drawn in, and finally the third agency was genuine and got me to London.

This is my story, but it's also a national one. More than a tenth of our population works abroad, and our government has adopted this as a formal economic strategy because, to be honest, remit-tances sent back by workers such as myself are the only thing that keeps the economy afloat. Stereo-types are generally derogatory, but if one of them happens to be positive then you can make money off it. Women from the Philippines have a reputa-tion for caring, patience, sensitivity and also docil-ity. If you have an elderly parent whom you love, but really can't give up your job to look after, and yet you don't want to send to a home for the elderly, then hiring a Filipina carer seems like an act of care in itself. You have carefully selected the person you think is most likely to possess the care and consid-eration that you would have liked to have given to your parent yet don't have time for yourself.

In the Philippines we know that we now have this reputation as premium carers, and that means we can charge a higher fee than carers from other coun-tries. So, if the push factor was poverty, the pull factor was this stereotype we could sell. I was one of the lucky ones ... and then became one of the very luckiest ones. It wasn't that long before I met Chris, got married, and was able to go back into education, and seven years later I too became a lecturer. That's hardly a common trajectory. During those years in care work, I met with hundreds of migrant labourers, from South India, West Africa and elsewhere. I know the sacrifices they make, struggles most Londoners can hardly begin to imagine. Filipina carers rarely get directly to the UK; most start in places such as Saudi and Hong Kong. Believe me, you don't want to be there when they tell stories of having been beaten and even raped. Unlike me, most of them have children they also have to leave behind in the Philippines.

I don't think a week goes by without the British press covering some story about migrants drowning at sea or dying inside sealed trucks in their desperation to get into Europe. Why do we all do this? You may think we represent the world's poorest. We don't. The really impoverished people in the Philippines simply don't have the money to invest in an individual migrant such as me. In fact I was unusual, since the key to my education was the scholarships. Most of my fellow migrants came from lower-middle-class groups who can invest in private education, nursing college and the agency fees for finding work abroad, or a scam student visa. So this is not an escape from starvation or an absolute lack of goods. But if you travel today to India or West Africa, to the family homes of any of these migrants, then it starts to make sense. Mostly, they may not have cars, but today they have motorbikes; they may not all have computers, but they all have mobile phones; a few have marble, but all can now afford decent houses with bathrooms.

Migrants rarely represent just themselves. Ask Chris about how often I continue to get requests from my family. The extended family that gave money to help you get here soon becomes the ever more extended family that demands the money you earn once you have settled. They all want to replace the motorbike with a car, to add a computer to the mobile phone, to eat out in restaurants, to take holidays, to have wide-screen televisions, big double fridges, and more fashionable clothes. I heard just yesterday that my father's brother, the one who sold that land to help me, has a nephew who wants a jeepney – a sort of extended taxi – to earn a living. When you accept a precarious passage on a leaky boat, suffer humiliation, take several simultaneous jobs, you are mindful not just of your own aspirations but often those of dozens of relatives – which I could meet thanks to a racist stereotype for compassion and patient care.

CHRIS: Well deserved in her case. We met when she was looking after my best friend's elderly parents, and I had never been in the presence of that kind of selfless dedication. I fell in love because I preached about such values, but Grace actually possessed them. Plus she was and still is gorgeous.

GRACE: I can now admit that I fell in love with the promise of an EU passport. Well, at first, but then subsequently with the man. But the real point is that most of my Filipino friends do domestic work inside houses just like this one, and we all come to the same conclusion. If you want to know what the English really think about consumption, ignore what they say, but look at what they do. Married to Chris, I now live in exactly that milieu which endlessly spins the story you just told about the urgent need to reduce consumption and waste. But the fact is I don't know a single, not one single individual who actually downsizes. Not one who doesn't live in a decent house – well, in your case, Mike, an actually delightful house, but also a fabulous garden in which I can see you take great pleasure – with vast numbers of books, ethnic furnishings and, yes, what people might well call conspicuous green consumer goods, organic goods and ecolabels, that we all know cost more than the nongreen variety. They discuss carbon footprints on flights to holidays in Australia. You complain about your son's aspirations, Mike, but from where most people in this world stand you are fabulously, unimaginably, wealthy.

MIKE: Well, yes, it's easy to accuse me of hypocrisy. But I never said I was living at the level we should be at. I agree it's not easy to downsize in practice, but I am quite sincere when I say I think this is unsustainable and everybody, including myself, needs to change.

GRACE: I wasn't about to accuse you of hypocrisy. But I do want to argue that the main change we need today is in the very opposite direction of what you have just argued for. I see an absolute need for that vast increase in consumption that you so fear. Because where we most part company is in terms of what we think consumption fundamentally is. The reason people don't want to go back to the Philippines is that, even if they can afford the house and the car and the clothes, what they would really miss from London are the basic services: the health system – it's the NHS above all that keeps migrant after migrant from going home – along with the education system they want to bequeath to their children, the transport system, the availability of leisure pursuits so that you can take your weekend hikes on protected pathways or stay with the unrivalled urban parks of London. There is the Indie music scene and the theatre. It is the public arena as much as private consumption. And, yes, the Philippines along with India and China want to build, need to build, hospitals, schools, road systems, heating and lighting and media systems, just the basic provisions you don't think about as consumption because you take them for granted. But it takes a hell of a lot of energy consumption to build a hospital.

The point I am making is that most of that extra consumption you fear will destroy the planet is not actually going to come from what you can claim to be surplus consumption, the hair gel and the jacuzzis. It will come from the provision of basic services that no one can call over-consumption. And we need to confront those, since they are a lot harder to curb. Even at British levels of consumption, who doesn't want to support the drive to have a local MRI scanner, a new drug for skin cancer that costs £73,000 per person per year, getting the bad schools up to the levels of the good ones, or retaining money for the arts and museums. It is no good taking advertising as your easy target. Not one of the demands I have just listed has anything to do with advertising or even with business. They are all governmental expenditures. You can attack ad men and capitalists and still feel good about your values. But the real energy consumption is going to come from the fact that every town in China and India wants a bus station and a hospital, and sooner or later they will get them.

But even if I come over to your agenda and what you consider over-consumption in the private domain, what do my family in the Philippines really, really want for themselves? Obvious things, actually: a well-built house with its bathrooms and garden, maybe not central heating, given the tropics, but the even more energy-consuming air conditioning. They want at least a single family car, a fridge-freezer and a washing machine. Would you do without a freezer – and you don't live in the tropics? You have a car even when your public transport system is infinitely better than ours. More subtle is the international spread in basic norms of comfort. There is the excellent work of the sociologist Elizabeth Shove[10] on how we come to regard as normal the number of times to wash in a week, or the right temperature of the water we wash with, or how we decide to set the thermostat for the cooling system of the building in which we work. These are at the heart of contemporary consumption statistics. But then it goes beyond even these so-called basic functional items. Why should my family not have as much right as yours to an annual holiday and a small range of household goods such as clothes, books, and access to the media – not just television, but increasingly mobile phones and computers that allow them to keep in touch with family living abroad, such as myself? Today, apart from a small fraction, pretty much the entire world population has come to see these not as basic goods, but as basic human rights, also as basic justice and equality.

Each time I go home on a visit I become more convinced that people who sacrifice their lives to gain remittances know what they are doing. I see families who never had hot water or a TV, whose children are the first in their family to get to university. These children want to discuss the same changes in Facebook or mobile phone apps that we talk about in London. They know more about Lady Gaga and Armani than most Londoners, but sometimes they also know more about Charles Dickens and human rights in Malaysia than I do. And I see the joy this brings their parents, who never ever dreamt this could possibly happen in one generation. I sit with these elderly parents and we cry – for joy. For those fortunate enough to gather what here seem the mere crumbs fallen from the tables of affluence, these are miracles. But this process has only begun. My problem is not at all that these children are becoming consumers. My problem is the hundreds of millions who still live without that access, who come to your TV screens as the parade of poverty.

CHRIS: Yes, but...

GRACE: I haven't finished yet. In fact, I now want to turn from Mike to you. In preparation for this meeting I spent the last two weeks (without telling you) monitoring every time you expressed what could be called a consumer desire. This is what I came up with: a better reclining chair for your back; some new kind of fan without blades; more affordable cashmere; less conspicuous fillings for your teeth next time you go to the dentist; a device that can automatically decide when headlights should come on, of the kind you spotted in Richard and Jean's car; an Android phone with a bigger screen; rice that cooks in two minutes in the microwave, for when I am out; more and better home insulation. And when you get some new gadget, does it disappoint you or show that you were a fool to desire it? Very rarely. I think you migrated from USB sticks to Dropbox and cloud computing nearly two years ago, and you still haven't stopped boring the world with its advantages – how your life is better because you were always losing those USB thingees.

CHRIS: Not having to carry a thumb drive is a real boon to us both. Remember the time we thought you had vacuumed one up and we had to...

GRACE: That's my point. I don't have your conservatism. I sometimes think the more radical you people claim to be in politics, the more conservative you are in practice. Of course cloud computing is better than a USB stick. But all these things are better. There was not a word of implicit criticism in that list (and, believe me, Mike, my husband gets plenty of criticism otherwise). I very occasionally do forget to switch on the car headlights, and that's dangerous. Why shouldn't you be able to afford cashmere? I suppose it might be safer for kids to have fans without blades – and of course that's the only reason you wanted one, wasn't it? We can live comfortably without all these things, but that doesn't make any of them bad. Other things being equal, new technologies are generally better than old ones.

MIKE: OK, but what about all that frankly totally useless extra crap that people buy, from electric pepper grinders to all those ornaments and silly bits of clothing that just seem waste? There is no way anyone will use them or needs them. Surely an anthropologist would at least condemn these?

GRACE: It's funny how green thinkers really don't get anthropology. You all seem to assume that buying useless stuff is a sign of how distant we are from the kinds of societies anthropologists traditionally study. Exactly the opposite is true. The whole point about non-capitalist societies is that they are not governed by mere utility. Material culture tends to be symbolic before it is functional. I teach about very long yams, decorated canoe prows, ear lobe extensions, temple architecture. One of our links to that aura of authentic society is that we remain interested in totally useless stuff, because useless stuff generally has a social and symbolic role. I remember a paper Alison Clarke[11] wrote about the 1950s examples of a genre called 'As seen on TV' – items such as the inside-the-shell egg scrambler, the Whip-o-Matic and the Hav-a-Maid – all of which turn out to have been absolutely central to gift-giving. Their only purpose was they worked quite well for Christmas or birthday presents and the like. But there is nothing more basic to anthropological concepts of what makes society than the gift-giving of symbolic goods.

CHRIS: And to summarise...

GRACE: All right, then, basically all this comes down to two points. The first is that, even if you could identify an arena of surplus goods, it would count for little because the vast majority of things that will lead to increases in consumption are basic infrastructure and goods we now all take for granted. But, even more importantly, I think you are making a fundamental mistake in conflating two quite different things. Let me be clear, I have no desire to detract from the fight to save the planet. I want you to succeed, I want us to succeed. But I think one of the main reasons you fail to have much impact upon consumption is because at the moment you rely on a claim that everyone in their daily behaviour contradicts, which is that a reduction in consumption is good for people. It's not good for people, except to the degree that it's good for the planet.

MIKE: But there is an imperative to cut back, and surely that forces us to create some kind of adjudication as to what objects we need more than others?

GRACE: But first you need to separate out arguments of necessity from those that imply a denigration of populations as being fooled by consumption. We might start to have a serious conversation about the environment when we admit that almost everything we would need to cut out is actually of direct benefit to human welfare or has symbolic value, and is desperately required for the entirely noble aim of reducing poverty or the sense of inequality. Dealing with climate change might actually mean cutting what the wealthy now regard as basic services and dashing the aspirations of most young people for still better health and education. After all, you are two grown men who last time we met were getting ridiculously over-excited by all those futuristic possibilities in *The Economist*'s *Technology Quarterly*.

MIKE: Actually half of those new technology gadgets were about how to save vast amounts of energy without the consequences you are talking about. They are exactly what you need to be considering given your arguments. But if this is now about being honest, then let's not pretend that you don't see us as a bunch of middle-class hypocrites. You clearly see me as some sort of green yuppie whose connoisseurship consists in searching out the ultimate eco-friendly, fair-trade goods from farmers' markets, which we consume at our dinner parties, and because they are more expensive than regular goods they thereby amount to some form of conspicuous consumption. Green is just the colour of privileged taste, is that it?

GRACE: No, no, honestly, no. That's not what I said, and I keep telling you it's not what I think. OK, maybe I was getting a bit carried away. But that is such an 'English' response; people here seem to have some sort of drive to embarrassment, the assumption that everyone is looking critically at their personal habits. I refuse to leave here and repay your hospitality by implanting such a notion. All my points were about your arguments, not your lifestyle. Actually I am the last person to accuse you of hypocrisy, but I admit that I now have a responsibility for spelling out exactly why. So grant me a few more minutes. In this case I suspect the problem comes from the very word 'consumption'.

Originally, to consume something means to use it up, in effect to destroy stuff. We think of a fire consuming a house. Two centuries ago consumption was associated with the dread of tuberculosis, a wasting disease. The contrast is with production, the work of artisans or artists, which adds stuff to the world. I have always seen a gender element to this. Chris's male proletariats make the world through their labour of production. Women use up the world through their labour of consumption.

CHRIS: I think that's Marx on labour, but actually the gender point seems fair.

GRACE: OK, but why does language do this – making production inherently good and consumption intrinsically evil?

MIKE: Well, given the impact of industrial and capitalist systems ...

GRACE: I figured you would think that. But you're wrong. It was true even in ancient times. So get ready for some anthropology. Whether you turn to ancient Greece or the Bible or pretty much any other ancient society, you will find that their cosmology was based on sacrifice, with incredible attention to the exact details of how to carry these out. There are several reasons for this,[12] but one clearly concerns the relationship between production and consumption. In fact many of these sacrifices are modelled on a kind of meal. The offering is consumed by fire, which lifts up the smoke as 'sweet savour' to the gods, leaving a now consecrated meal eaten in a way that sanctified the social order. For example, priests eat their share, followed by commoners. Then look at what they sacrificed. Typically the Bible talks of first fruits, or the newly born but unblemished lambs. So human beings thereby acknowledge the divinity as the true source of production. The first perfect produce is returned to its originator, and only then can humans consume the rest. Merely to consume would be to use up the world without first ensuring its constant replenishment through divine intervention.

So the first exchange is with the divine. The second is with other people. If we just consume what we grow, that is a very small circle. So many societies prohibit that. What we produce gets exchanged with others. In anthropology we teach that it is exchange that is the bedrock for our social relationships, through mutual obligation to return the debt. Once goods have been exchanged with the divine and used to create these relationships, then it's OK to consume them. If we merely consume without all this exchange, we lose the opportunity to create our cultural worlds with those products. I think that's why the idea of mere consumption was always seen so negatively. This is not just some weird eccentric idea; it seems to be common to almost all past and many contemporary societies.

So, Mike, when you and your fellow middle-class Londoners sit around your dinner table complaining about how everyone is materialistic and consumes too much, what you are doing is confirming your proper moral values before you actually go ahead and consume anything. In the more ritualised setting of your dinner parties, you *should* have exactly that conversation before you can eat. The reason I would never ever accuse you of hypocrisy is that I would argue you are enacting a ritual that goes back thousands of years and is perhaps the most basic ritual in human existence.

MIKE: Wow! I mean, wow. I have to say I didn't see that coming. The entire world has been telling us that our middle-class dinner parties are the very essence of shallow, and then you come along and discern in them the most fundamental and ancient of ritual acts. Isn't anthropology wonderful?

GRACE: You're welcome. But while you are basking in that, I can complete my argument. My point is that, from the beginnings of history, we have used the critique of consumption to confirm ourselves as essentially good and moral beings. Once upon a more religious time it was common to translate this into an actual asceticism, and I still think it gives us reason to lash out against a consumption we can't seem to control even in ourselves.

MIKE: Any other impacts?

GRACE: Well, for example, I might have expected most of your green venom to be directed against the destruction of the world's resources associated with production, such as the impact of heavy industry or agro-industry rather than consumption. After all, these are the main sources of pollution. But in the colloquial environmentalism of the London dinner party, somehow it has to take the form of mea culpa. You the individual sinner who forgot your recycling bags were in the boot of the car. It is your personal fault that the planet is overheating.

MIKE: Actually...

GRACE: Sorry, I was just trying to answer your question. But I am interrupting because I have already taken more than my fair share of time and I still haven't got to my book. But hopefully this background was useful, since the book is actually called *Excess: Anti-Consumerism in the West*, by Kim Humphrey.[13] Rather like you, Mike, the people he discusses tend to see climate change almost as some kind of moral retribution for the crime of succumbing to affluenza[14] – the disease of over-consumption. He deals with a swathe of public intellectuals who take this position, such as Zygmunt Bauman and Juliet Schor,[15] but he also did fieldwork among much less well-known anti-consumer activists. He clearly admires those who don't just pontificate but are really trying to do something about over-consumption. Much of the contents of their arguments will be familiar enough. They also overlap with your position on how wealth does not bring happiness, on the need to decide how much is enough, on how an American sees 3,000 adverts a day, or how consumption is addictive. The field ranges from more philosophical arguments, such as Kate Soper[16] thinking about alternative models for citizenship, through to a dozen variants of post-Marxist critiques of 'the system'. He shares your feeling that climate change has to be at the top of our agenda and that we have an urgent need to consider not just how and why we consume, but also how much we consume.

MIKE: Sounds like my kind of guy. Still, if you chose him I am guessing there is a 'yes...but'.

GRACE: Quite so. Because, by the end of the book, I found that Humphrey had reinforced all my prejudices against these movements. He notes that so many of their arguments are not just repetitive but very poorly backed up academically. There is very little evidence behind the contentions, partly because many of them are quite suspicious of science. In fact they tend to do exactly what that book by Hulme seems to suggest we all do, which is to make climate change debates into a cover or legitimation for what are really much more ideological oppositions to consumption itself, as capitalist, or vulgar or materialistic. The anti-consumer activists constantly contradict each other, on the one hand bitterly opposed to economic liberalism and its ideal of unlimited individual choice, and yet making these criticisms in the name of a pretty much identical liberalism of individual personal freedom from business or the state.

Like you, these activists see a world of over-consumption that is ultimately detrimental to our humanity or to our soul. But, much more than you, they constantly deride the mass population of ordinary consumers as stupid and deluded, assuming that they buy things out of regard for advertising and commercial pressure. But it's always the same. These few green activists are 'the saved', the enlightened who have seen the truth. But, as far as I am concerned, any movement based on the idea that most people are stupid and deluded is itself thoroughly deluded.

MIKE: But even if one was to accept your point about decoupling our concern with the planet from this wider moralism, surely you agree that we have lost an essential respect for nature itself?

GRACE: Actually I am even less inclined to go in that direction. It's just another example of the same problem. This word 'nature', when used to imply outside of culture, is a mythic idyll. People who live close to the environment don't try to live in harmony with nature, quite the opposite. A few generations ago we had far fewer means to resist nature, and the result was a very low life expectancy, much of which was spent wracked by disease. Death is natural, disease is natural; most nature programmes consist of one animal eating another one alive. We have known since Darwin that the morality underpinning evolution is survival of the fittest. The whole point of humanity as any kind of moral order is the struggle to overcome nature. So, for me, nature and morality are the very antithesis of each other. Though don't assume my views are typical of anthropology – anything but.

MIKE: Now I think you're getting silly. What about landscapes? Aren't they beautiful?

GRACE: Most are not natural. Have you any idea how gloomy it is under true tropical forest? Almost every landscape you walk in and admire is the result of human cultivation and, these days, often a quite deliberate aesthetic of landscaping. OK, I don't want to exaggerate. I too will be entranced by waves crashing on rocks. I adore David Attenborough, and, yes, I feel we have a moral responsibility for saving species diversity. But I insist that my values come from a morality which humanity formed in opposition to nature. Look, whether you agree with that doesn't matter. What does matter is when – and this does happen, especially among ordinary consumers – you can feel green ideology descending into a hopeless mishmash of actual environmental problems, pseudo-religious asceticism and romantic projections upon nature. If you really feel cutting energy usage is the priority, then buying supermarket meals which are created centrally is more energy efficient than every household cooking its own meals,[17] but I can't see that on the green menu.

What I also see in these cults of nature and asceticism is continuity with the older elitist distaste for mass culture, where mass consumption is regarded as vulgar and shallow, the almost visceral loathing of McDonald's. You should see the way people look at me when sometimes I deliberately come to work in the clothes I used to wear when I worked as a carer – fake Victoria Beckham jeans and a blouse studded with Swarovski crystals. Then we Filipina women are viewed as lurid, vulgar and cheap. Bad consumption is of course lower-class consumption.

CHRIS: Did I hear the word class? Hallelujah – we have a sort of marital agreement that that's my cue for interruption. I am the 'class' act in this marriage.

GRACE: Well, you are clearly the corny act in this marriage. But, to be fair, I have had more than my two cents by now. Even I can sense that I have headed off towards rant. When I get into my thing about nature, everyone decides I am just a crank. So go for it.

CHRIS: Gosh, I can't remember the last time I ended up as the final speaker in a debate. But that's fine. I am now in the perfect position to sort you two out. Plus it means Mike can have some more of the ube he has been eyeing up and Grace can finally have a beer.

MIKE: Oh, I am sorry, I meant to offer.

CHRIS: Not at all. I didn't mean to insinuate otherwise. The beer is on the table, we just needed a pause. Let me just say again how happy I am that you invited us. You might think, because we both teach about consumption, that this is our pillow talk. Actually, while we do go on about work when we are at home, it is almost always to do with administrative idiocy, government cuts and grant proposals. It is very rarely the actual content of our academic research and ideas. I think Grace feels that home should be a refuge from my endless propensity to debate, but then today we are not at home.

Listening to you both, I felt that, while we are all social scientists, so far there really hasn't been that much social science. In the end Mike's argument comes down to an assertion that, from the perspective of the planet, we have to decrease consumption, and Grace's story amounts to an argument that, from the perspective of most of the people of the planet, we have to increase consumption. But we haven't really started to engage in why we consume, and we haven't really put consumption back into the study of social relations. I think by doing so we might resolve some of your problems and differences. I have seen and can bear witness to all that Grace described about her home and family. She hasn't exaggerated at all. But I think her emotional and personal involvement has kept her from a more analytical perspective.

GRACE: Just how many minutes does it take before my husband turns into a condescending little...

CHRIS (quickly interrupting): Which is curious, because if you want to do what Grace intends and look at the historical roots of our conversation, then actually the critique of consumption has always been associated with social hierarchy. You mentioned the ancient world, but, whether it is Juvenal's satires or early Greek drama, consumption was also strongly associated with the critique of luxury by the poor and of vulgarity by the wealthy. Pretty much my all-time favourite book on consumption, and the one I use in the first lecture to my undergraduates, is called *Courtesans and Fishcakes*, by James Davidson.[18] It shows just how important it was in ancient Greece to develop a measured relationship to consumption between asceticism and greed and how this becomes central to the development of the Greek *polis* and democracy more generally. These remain big issues in the development of Christianity and subsequent literature and politics. The core focus on consumption as an expression of social difference is provided by academic analysis which stems mostly from Veblen's classic *The Theory of the Leisure Class*,[19] the book which gave rise to much of our current language with regard to consumption, from the concept of *conspicuous consumption* to the *keeping up with the Joneses*, based on the principle of emulation. Veblen had a huge popular impact, and his ideas continue to dominate anti-consumption rhetoric in US writings.[20] What really upset Veblen was not the traditional aristocracy, but the nouveau riche, because the latter made their money in what he saw as proper industry, but then would emulate the kinds of effete appearance and clothing that entirely denied the roots of that wealth in labour. Veblen was enraged by this betrayal of the foundational American Puritan ideals, where industry should be respected and acknowledged as a proper source of wealth.

There are remarkably few developments in consumption theory between Veblen and the 1970s. Then the anthropologist Mary Douglas, while working at University College London, applied structural analysis to consumption.[21] For example, she once argued that there was progressive geometricisation and desiccation through the day in working-class meals, from cereals with milk, to meat with gravy, to cake with custard.[22]

GRACE: Doesn't it end with geometric biscuits and icing or some such? Did you finish your day with a nice custard cream dunked in your Horlicks?

CHRIS: The details don't matter. The idea was that consumption was a symbolic system we use but we don't understand, in the same way that we speak language clearly without being able to give a lesson in grammar. At the same time, Western Marxism was developing its critique of class relations, and the two come together in the work of the sociologist Pierre Bourdieu.

GRACE: Anthropologist.

CHRIS: Sociologist.

GRACE: Anthropologist!

CHRIS: Sorry, Mike, actually we have bonded over our common love of Bourdieu, but never agreed to divide him between our disciplines. Anyway, whatever he was, in his book *Distinction*[23] Bourdieu refuted the idea that consumer taste was a personal individual preference, showing instead the way it maps quite precisely onto class relationships. So the social inequality foregrounded by Marxism works as the symbolic system of difference foregrounded by Douglas. In Bourdieu's book, the taste of working-class people is for food that evidently fills you up when are hungry, like roast beef and potatoes or fish and chips. This reflects the fact that they make a living through manual labour. The wealthy, meanwhile, are divided into those with financial capital, who naturally like their rich sauces and truffles, as against those with aesthetic capital, who prefer nouvelle cuisine, a minimal food that, in direct opposition to the situation of the working class, seems to deny that we actually eat food because we need it. The middle class have their own moral capital, reflected in the taste for organics and fair trade – the echinacea-flavoured wholemeal pasta I suspect lurks somewhere in Mike's cupboard.

MIKE: Wait a minute – echinacea-flavoured wholemeal pasta? That *is* below the belt.

Bourdieu

CHRIS: Sorry, sorry, sorry! Couldn't resist, but the point is
            that each group disdains the other as vulgar or
            pretentious or whatever, so taste is really a map of
            structural differences between classes.

GRACE: To be honest, Chris, you *are* being rude to Mike,
            but it's not by casting aspersions on the inside of
            his cupboards. It's by treating us all to your first-
            year lectures. I am sure Mike knows Douglas and
            Bourdieu just as well as we do.

MIKE: Thank you, Grace. Actually, Chris, you do seem to
            have forgotten that I too teach consumption studies.

CHRIS: Of course. Oh dear, yes, I do tend to revert to
            lecture mode.[24] OK, let's take our knowledge of
            older approaches as given. Actually, all I wanted to
            do in that mini-review was to demonstrate the cen-
            trality of social difference to the study of consump-
            tion from ancient to modern times, in order to
            introduce the book I brought with me to discuss,
            and to which, duly chastened, I shall now most
            swiftly turn. It is called *The Spirit Level*, by Richard
            Wilkinson and Kate Pickett.[25]

            I didn't think I was going to like *The Spirit Level*,
            since it starts by citing one of those books about
            happiness. I confess I am just as sceptical about
            these as Grace. When it comes to cultural differ-
            ences, even I can see that, if the Irish seem among
            the happiest people on the planet and the Russians
            among the most miserable, the reasons may be
            other than income or, for that matter, alcohol. As
            someone who has studied poverty in the UK, when
            I read a book that says happiness has not increased
            since the 1950s, all that tells me is to avoid books
            that tackle happiness through questionnaires.[26]

GRACE: In my village it was a badge of honour to claim you
            were happy when you were really struggling, while
            today I have been to enough North London dinner
            parties to know that to stand up and say you are
            happy is completely unsophisticated. It makes you
            look complacent and incapable of engaging in
            proper critical dialogue. The way some of Chris's

friends look at my Filipina friends, you can tell that to be happy is to be vulgar. I suspect that's the reason why, the wealthier you are, the less likely you may be to claim happiness.

CHRIS: Meanwhile, back at the book, after the first few pages the authors turn to rather more specific and, to my mind, more acceptable measures based on health and quantifiable aspects of welfare. What the book sets out to prove, and, in my opinion, indisputably does prove, is that inequality is bad for everyone. At first what gives people improved health is the escape from poverty and basic development but, once a certain level is reached, the marked discrepancy is between countries with the same amount of wealth.

At the core of the book lies a whole series of graphs. These come in two basic versions. The first compares over twenty countries, and the other compares all the individual states in the United States. One variable in all these graphs is the degree of social inequality within each country or within each US state. This is set against a range of measurements of health and welfare. The second set of graphs takes the average income of these countries and US states and sets it against the same range of measurements of health and welfare. So, for example, in the first data chapter they look at three criteria: overall health, social problems and children's wellbeing. The graphs show no alignment at all between any of these against average income, but a strong and clear association against internal degrees of social inequality.

The point they are making is that, intuitively, we would think that a richer country or a richer US state with more resources would fare better in relation to factors such as health, social problems and children's wellbeing. But these graphs show clearly that richer countries or richer US states do no better than poorer ones. By contrast, those countries and US states with a more equal distribution of wealth do far better on all these measures than those with high degrees of inequality. The conclusion is stark and clear. I quote: 'Differences in average income or living standards between whole populations or countries don't matter at all, but income differences within those same populations matter very much indeed.'[27]

The pattern is then repeated for pretty much any variable where they can get sufficiently robust statistics for testing. These range from levels of obesity to educational attainment, from trust in others to infant mortality, from levels of violence to social mobility, from the amount of imprisonment to teenage pregnancies. In every case it is the degree of inequality that correlates with these differences, not the amount of wealth. The most extraordinary results in this book come when they show that even the rich in rich countries suffer from inequality. For example, the poorest people in Sweden still have better rates of infant mortality than the wealthiest people in the UK. Thus the subtitle of their book: 'Why equality is better for everyone'.

There is quite a topical argument in relation to something I saw in today's papers about 'the Big Society' in the UK. There is a strong argument within the book that growth in inequality leads to a lack of trust, which leads to a decline in participation in communal activity. In 2011 the UK coalition government wanted to cut welfare and replace it by volunteering and civil participation in what they called the Big Society. But actually what they are doing is increasing social inequality, which is what inevitably leads to a decline in such participation and shrinkage in that Big Society. They have the whole thing back to front. To be honest, there is very little about consumption in this book, but I think it has considerable relevance. For example, a cartoon[28] shows large and ostentatious shopping bags that say things like 'Bet you wish you could afford this stuff', because it is conspicuous consumption expressing inequality that stimulates emulation and greed.

MIKE: I have been with you so far, but now you are really starting to worry me. One of the problems with this emphasis upon social inequality is the way it gets taken up in economics. I recently went to a talk by Robert Skidelsky,[29] one of my favourite economists, but like so many in his discipline he also seemed to assume that the problem with inequality is that it promotes Veblen-style emulation and the drive to consume, which is all about greed, stimulated by those who have more than we do. This is one of the great clichés about consumption. But it simply assumes that we all have this natural tendency towards avarice and jealousy. I think there is an alternative explanation. I was struck when Grace was talking earlier about the aspirations of her family in the Philippines. Clearly the vast gulf in income has nothing to do with people working hard, being more entrepreneurial, having differential ability or getting what they deserve. It is sheer chance that one person is born to a farmer in the Philippines and the other to an academic in London.

This reminded me of another book I read recently, which was *The Idea of Justice*, by Amartya Sen.[30] Sen's topic is what he calls redressable injustices. He starts by noting how adults are just as hurt by manifest unfairness as are children. If inequality leads to a desire for greater wealth, I suspect the main motivation is not greed or jealousy, but unhappiness at the manifest unfairness this represents. It is the evidence that other people possess wealth mainly for no good reason other than the chance of birth. I agree with Sen: adults are just as upset by this as children, though a cultural system such as caste can naturalise and thus neutralise inequality by representing it as fair in some larger cosmological or Karmic scheme, where this represents reward and punishment for behaviour in some past life.

GRACE: I certainly see all this within my own family. In general in the Philippines we do accept differentiation based on meritocracy, but we just can't bear the way we work hard and intelligently for so little and see these lazy idiots flaunting their wealth. I guess Mike's point is not a criticism of *The Spirit Level*, just a pre-emptive strike against drawing the wrong conclusions.

CHRIS: OK, I think I can concede that point. Maybe *The Spirit Level* is wrong to assume envy as a primary cause, and, as I said, consumption is not really Wilkinson and Pickett's topic. But this shouldn't detract from the main argument. What to me *The Spirit Level* demonstrates is that social science needs to look at consumption in terms of the way it expresses relationships rather than as a mere increase in technical capacity. Actually, it builds on Grace's point about the symbolic quality of goods. Goods used to mark social difference can become debilitating to all, even to the rich who employ them in that manner. If we want to improve social welfare and individual wellbeing, we need to get off that treadmill and instead concentrate on reducing social inequality. This is not some antiquated diehard socialism, which I know you think is all I ever spout. This book doesn't require any particular political position. In fact, contrary to my own politics, this book doesn't favour state involvement. The authors see benefits in equality even if this occurs at the level of initial income rather than through state distribution. So maybe Grace needs to be more concerned with the politics of the Philippines – an old-style oligarchy where wealthy landowning families always remain in power and inequality is rife – rather than going on about whether her family has a washing machine.

GRACE: You're so wrong. Look, you made me read *The Spirit Level*, and I got a lot out of it, and your summary is accurate as far as it goes. But – and it's a big but – if you look at those graphs again you will find that they are all of affluent societies, and those US states. The only countries they include from Asia are Japan, Australia and New Zealand. So most of the world is excluded. It says nothing about the Philippines. Even the authors acknowledge that. So we have a long way to go before we even reach your playing field. Meanwhile, we still need washing machines. Meanwhile, you forgot that your attack on Philippine oligarchy, which has preserved detestable levels of inequality, actually comes from me. Why do males have this infernal habit of spouting back to the same females who gave them their information, and just assume they will be credited with it?

CHRIS: Yes, of course, critiques of the Philippines do come from you, and, yes, I do have that tendency. But equally, yes – the authors do concede that first we have to tackle absolute poverty. But I still think this book has really significant consequences for our arguments. The key is those affluent countries such as the US and the UK. We are the main polluters, and we set the standards that places such as India and China are bound to look to. Unless we change, just telling them to aim for different goals is asking to be dismissed as hypocrites.

MIKE: Listen, I have been thinking that we have reached the stage where we have all spoken to the books we brought and said something about 'where we are coming from'.

GRACE: Well, Chris didn't.

MIKE: True, but still I think maybe we need to wind up. What if we set an instant rule that each of us can make one final point. To be honest, we need to progress to some practical consumption of the dinner we have prepared for you, where you can meet my family.

CHRIS: Oh, sorry, I guess we weren't sure what the time-scale was. Of course that would be just fine. Actually I suppose I could even make my final point into my missing 'where I am coming from'.

GRACE: Where you are coming from? I sometimes think you were born in Highgate cemetery, somewhere between Karl Marx and Herbert Spencer, the social evolutionists who are buried a few metres from each other.

CHRIS: Oh no, not the old Marks and Spencer joke! But Grace well knows I remain pretty unrepentant when it comes to my education in the writings of Karl Marx. The authors of *The Spirit Level* avoid all mention of Marx and socialism. I am guessing it's because they think that will lead to the glib dismissal of their case and also because they separate inequality from state redistribution. But that is where we part company. Underlying *The Spirit Level* is a system of class that remains pernicious and fosters inequality, while portraying itself as the competitive aspiration required by markets. When I go on about capitalism you treat me like some kind of dinosaur that forgot to evolve. But I refuse to accept that this is some kind of anachronism. After all, we have a lesson right to hand. Two years ago we suffered a catastrophic banking crisis affecting people from all over the world. Yet so powerful are the ideological forces that bolster the capitalist system that, instead of our all being concerned with irresponsible financial systems and overpaid executives, both of which remain largely in place, we are using that crisis as an excuse to cut public expenditure, turn more of that sector over to the market and thereby further increase inequality. We get screwed by the market, and in response we become still more compliant to its bidding.

So my final point comes direct from the heart of old-fashioned Marxism, which wore this heart on its sleeve. I want to end by linking back to Mike's environmental interests. Grace and I went to the book launch of *Out of this Earth*, a devastating critique of the global aluminium industry and the destruction and impoverishment of indigenous people in India.[31] More recently we heard a lecture by Arundhati Roy,[32] again pointing out that, for all the rise of the middle classes in India, there is a huge lag of unremitting poverty and unregulated environmental destruction. Both the causes and the consequences of consumption lie in these same global systems that are deeply involved in the destruction caused by the exploitation of our planet's resources. Look at the fate of those who are unfortunate enough to be living in places affected by bauxite extraction, aluminium smelters and all the other detritus of that industry. It's not about some cult worship of nature, Grace. It's that we still live in a world where violent attacks on nature remain associated with violent attacks on any population that gets in the way of these forces. As far as I am concerned, a student who is not brought face to face with such suffering can never be said to have been educated in the consequences of consumption.

GRACE: You can see, Mike, why it's hard to argue with Chris. Who would not want to be associated with the underlying humanity and sense of justice that has become the bedrock to his beliefs? I have no desire to forget the persistence of poverty among my own relatives in the Philippines. Within anthropology we are constantly reminded of our specific responsibilities for the protection of vulnerable indigenous populations, and we are in an ideal position to see those global connections between consumption, poverty and underdevelopment. It is just that – and I suppose this is my final point – I can no longer accept his assumption that these problems can be resolved merely through the critique of capitalism itself. I have come to see that trying to deal with specific acts of injustice and oppression are just not helped by trying to make them an instance of such an overgeneralised term as capitalism.

Chris says that we can't dissociate demand for consumption from forces such as advertising and commerce more generally. However, until relatively late in its development, the Soviet bloc had very little advertising but ever more pent-up demand.[33] I simply don't believe that capitalism is the reason my family wants goods. The richest countries have historically been Scandinavian welfare-driven social democracies with one of the most controlled versions of competition-driven capitalism. The thing is that, by blaming capitalism for wealth, you also credit capitalism with the spread of wealth, and that has been the undoing of the left.

MIKE: Well, I think the dispute between you two is pretty clear and seems to remain impressively compatible with marriage. What worries me is that we have now got to the social context of consumption, but so far we have barely dealt with social difference, and I can see a million other things we might turn to, ranging from gender and cultural difference to the impact of new digital technologies. We said we would try and deal today with what consumption is, but how far do you really think we have got?

GRACE: OK, then I have a suggestion. I teach in the Department of Anthropology at UCL, where Douglas once taught. Danny Miller, the colleague who recruited me, has a book coming out summarising a lot of the ethnographic research he has conducted on precisely that topic. One of the advantages of his ethnographic focus is that I think he genuinely tries to come to terms with consumption in its own right. By contrast, I feel our arguments, including my own, keep reducing consumption to something else.

CHRIS: Well, Miller's work has been another source of mild marital dissent, but Grace claims that at least this one is going to be more readable than some of the others.

MIKE: OK, fine. If you can send us the draft I am happy to read it. But then let's take that as a done deal, because I want us to get to what, for me at any rate, is the payoff. We said before that in our next meeting we would commit to seeing whether, individually or collectively, we could come up with some feasible contributions to the immediate issue of how understanding consumption helps us deal with the consequences of consumption and, most especially, the issue of climate change.

GRACE: Well, not just climate change. Miller also takes the political economy itself as a consequence rather than, as most people would, the cause of consumption.

MIKE: No problem: all the more reason to read it.

CHRIS: One condition. Next time you must come over to us and get acquainted with a couple of unusual beers I think you might enjoy.

GRACE: And I might just manage to have made some more ube by then.

MIKE: Brilliant. Look forward to it. Meanwhile, dinner awaits.

2

A Consumer Society

The next four chapters comprise the 'book' that Chris, Grace and Mike have gone away to read. Each chapter is a summary of previously published work. The first three are concerned to establish what consumption is and what its more direct consequences for society, families and individuals might be. So chapter 3 is a study of shopping, as the acquisition of goods, and the consequences of shopping, mainly for families, though also the wider ethical issues. Chapter 4 focuses upon denim blue jeans. It tries to answer the simple question of why we buy so many blue jeans and then enumerates a range of consequences that follow that choice. Chapter 5 looks at the connections to and consequences for the wider political economy. We then return in the final chapter to our three protagonists, who argue the implications for climate change.

The intention of the current chapter is to look at what happens when an island becomes a consumer society and examines four aspects of that process. It starts with a consideration of the growing role of objects as goods in expressing the values of that society. A study of Coca-Cola asks whether this means that the island is being swamped by and homogenised into a global commodity culture.[1] This leads to a short, more theoretical excursion in the third section. I argue that these research findings should lead us to question the most common, rather dismissive, approach to consumption in social science. Rather than seeing consumers merely as the passive end point of economic activity, I argue that they actively transform their world. They too see both the negative and the positive consequences of consumption and have their own critiques. So the final section on Christmas becomes an example of this. It shows both how the people of Trinidad identify materialism as one of the problematic consequences of the rise of consumption and one of the ways in which they try to deal with this problem. Taken together, this chapter addresses several of the key consequences of a society becoming a consumer society. By 'consumer society', I mean one in which commodities are increasingly used to express the core values of that society but also become the principal form through which people come to see, recognise and understand those values.

Anyone for a Coke?

Why did I go to Trinidad[2] in order to study consumption? Should I be really honest and admit how much listening to David Rudder's *Calypso Music* played a part, and that once I got there I discovered that a Trini fete just has to be one of the best parties in the world? No, perish the thought. The grounds were entirely academic. As an oil-boom country, Trinidad lurched with extraordinary speed from being a developing state, before the 1970s, to the status of the third richest country in the Americas, briefly during the 1970s, to having lost most of this wealth by the late 1980s. Anthropologists argue that we tend to take our own world for granted, and, having been a consumer society for such a long time, it is difficult for us to gaze insightfully at the nature and implications of our own consumption. I was hoping that these rapid changes meant that, for Trinidadians, the distinctions between a consumer-rich and consumer-poor society were still fairly fresh. The other reason was my conviction that you couldn't study consumption without also studying the world of commerce that produced the goods, which was a lot to try and accomplish in one study. It might help that Trinidad is a relatively small island – you can drive around it in one day.

My intention was to establish a more specifically anthropological perspective on consumption. This meant not starting with the individual, as would have been the case in the dominant disciplines of economics and psychology, but thinking in terms of a larger population. What does it mean for a whole country to become a consumer society, not just for an individual to be a consumer? Fortunately, one of the most accomplished of modern fiction writers had posed my research question rather neatly. V. S. Naipaul was brought up in the town of Chaguanas in central Trinidad, and his response to the emergence of his country as a consumer society was eloquently expressed in the title of his book *The Mimic Men*.[3] For Naipaul, Trinidad was quintessentially a consumer society because all it produced was oil, something quite hard to feel any particular relationship to as a product. Almost all of its consumer goods were imported in exchange for oil. At the time of my initial research (1987–9) Trinidad grew a smaller proportion of its own food than did the UK. So the sense of end user that follows from the word consumer seemed to extend to the whole society. *The Mimic Men* suggests a prime example of an inauthentic consumer-driven society. Even the people had originally come from elsewhere; around 40 per cent were descended from African slaves and 40 per cent from South Asian indentured labour. There was no clear remaining indigenous population. The implication of an imported people importing their culture in the form of commodities was that there could be no originality here. As Grace noted in the last chapter, production, like labour, art and design, is seen as adding to the world. Consumption merely uses the world up. The key scenes for Naipaul were of post-modern frippery: a swimming pool next to something that looked like a Roman villa, a bastard hodge-podge in pale imitation of real worlds that lay elsewhere.

The idea that peripheral countries are merely mimics of a more authentic metropolitan consumer culture leading to an overall global homogenisation seems to be affirmed most clearly by the spread of key brands, often of US origin, such as Coca-Cola and McDonald's. I can no longer count the times I have listened to anthropologists complaining that the world of authentic diversity was evidently diminished now they had seen Coca-Cola being drunk by shamans in New Guinea or Amazonia. So let's take up this specific challenge. Perhaps the best place to start an ethnographic investigation is to tackle these head on and ask the question of how far Trinidad is indeed an example of Coca-Globalisation.[4] What actually does it mean to see someone drinking a bottle of Coca-Cola in Trinidad?

There is a category of drink in Trinidad known as the sweet drink, which corresponds to what in the UK is called a soft or fizzy drink. When I was a child I recall drinking both an apple- and a pear-flavoured fizzy drink, known respectively as Cydrax and Peardrax. These have subsequently disappeared from the UK, and today about the only place in the world where they are still available is in fact Trinidad and Tobago, where they have come to occupy a particular niche. Cydrax and Peardrax are considered the premium sweet drinks. They are particularly favoured by teetotal Indo-Trinidadians as a substitute for champagne at celebrations such as weddings. They cost slightly more than other sweet drinks. Curiously, none of this was true of these drinks in their original market within the UK. It seems that drinks can behave a little like Darwin's finches. Having migrated to a new island, they find a previously uncolonised niche, and adapt to fit that niche. Unlike the finches, a drink cannot evolve new features such as a beak or claw, but rather it may develop new symbolic properties that define it as something different from its previous version. So today these are clearly Trinidadian drinks that we can understand only from the perspective of Trinidadian culture.

This example opens up two very different scenarios for an investigation of Coca-Cola. On the one hand, we can see Coke as the quintessential American drink whose colonisation of this island remains significant essentially as a form of Americanisation. To the degree that Trinis drink Coke, they become more like the Americans and everyone else that drinks Coke, losing something of their cultural specificity and becoming merely an example of global homogenisation. Alternatively, there is at least the theoretical possibility that Coke is more like Darwin's finch – that, once it migrates, it adapts to the new environment to such an extent that it is actually better understood as a sign of the very opposite phenomenon, the capacity to regenerate cultural difference and diversity.

One version of the first hypothesis, that of cultural homogenisation, tends to see all such consumer goods as reflections of the companies that own them; they are merely the outward sign of the hidden forces of the global corporation. Coke is not just the

US; it is really Atlanta, its home town, that spreads its sticky black syrup across the world.[5] At one level this must be true. Coke has always retained its underlying recipe as a closely guarded secret. No one else is allowed to make this syrup, which is indeed exported to most countries in the world from Atlanta. The corporation is also fierce in guarding its logo and associated style; any local advertising company has to get clearance from Atlanta before it makes any changes to the aesthetics of Coke. On the other hand, the syrup is all that Coca-Cola exports. Perhaps surprisingly, Coke is often a franchise operation. In most cases the actual shift from syrup to drink and the subsequent bottling is done by a local company, which pays only for the syrup itself. In most countries that might not matter very much, but Trinidad is very small and there aren't many bottling companies, and pretty much everyone knows their names and their reputations. Coke in Trinidad is bottled by Cannings, a company within the Neil & Massy group. This has a very specific reputation, representing the largest of the old colonial firms associated with the French Creole population. In fact, at the time of my fieldwork it was the biggest multinational in the Caribbean. It would have been very different if Coke had been produced by a Trinidadian 'Chinese' company, such as L. J. Williams (who made Peardrax), or an 'Indian' company, such as Solo or Jaleel. So, even at the level of its production Coke seems to be a bit more of a finch than we might have guessed.

When we talk of the power of capitalist corporations, we might assume that the one element over which they have indisputable control would be their own products. But, again, a closer look at Coke suggests otherwise. In the 1980s Coca-Cola was worried by the increasing market share being gained by its key rival, Pepsi, and in response it changed the flavour, making it a bit sweeter and more like Pepsi. The trouble was that the general public in the US was not prepared to accept this change in what had become a hallowed tradition, and the company was soon forced to back-track and restore the original flavour. This suggests that a corporation does not necessarily entirely control even its own goods.

Once we start to examine the situation in Trinidad, we again find that Coke is inseparable from its particular history in the region. Certainly Coke came in with the US, especially the US military in the Second World War, but it quickly became associated with the quite specific combination of 'rum and Coke', which locally, along with Carib beer, became seen as the most quintessentially Trinidadian form of alcohol consumption. As such, Coke soon came to represent not the acceptance of American culture but, surprisingly, the local resistance to US culture. Perhaps the most famous song ever to come out of Trinidad was the calypso called *Rum and Coca-Cola*, complemented by a local novel with the same title. The song, with its reprise 'mother and daughter working for the Yankee dollar', is concerned primarily to critique the rise of prostitution associated with serving the visiting US military. This finch seems to be growing claws in its new niche.

When consumed independently from rum, Coke migrates from being a soft drink to becoming a 'sweet drink', at which point we clearly need to understand the local ecology of sweet drinks. In Trinidad most such drinks have evolved into two basic and opposed categories. There is today the red sweet drink and the black sweet drink. The red drink is the quintessential sweet drink in as much as it is considered by consumers to be the drink highest in sugar content. The Indian population is generally assumed to be particularly fond of sugar and sweet products. This in turn is supposed to relate to their entry into Trinidad largely as indentured labourers in the sugar-cane fields. They are also thought to have a high rate of diabetes, which folk wisdom claims to be a result of their over-indulgence of these preferences. Today, adverts which provide images of consumption will most often refer to a 'red and a roti' as the proper combination. The implication here is that non-Indians also would most appropriately take a red drink with their roti when eating out, since the roti has become a general 'fast food' item which appeals to all communities within Trinidad.

While both red and black sweet drinks are drunk by all people from all ethnic groups, they are still seen as having ethnic connotations. Thus an Indo-Trinidadian talked of seeing Coke as a more 'white' and 'white-oriented people' drink. The term 'white-oriented', however, is here a synonym for Afro-Trinidadians. Many Indians assume that Africans have a much greater aptitude for emulating white taste and customs, in order to become what is locally termed 'Afro-Saxons'. Africans, in turn, would refute this accusation and claim that, while they lay claim to white culture, Indians are much more deferential. The key point, though, is that Coke has become in effect the premium black sweet drink, so that, when I would visit someone's house, if they had more money they would bring me out a Coke, if less money then it would be a generic black sweet drink. Among a community of low-income squatters where I worked, people would just go to a bar and say 'gimme a black' or 'gimme a red'. Clearly one is literally drinking in Trinidadian cultural dualism.

The semiotic relationship may or may not become explicit. One of the most successful local advertising campaigns in the sweet drink industry to occur during my period of fieldwork was for Canada Dry, which was marketed not as a ginger ale, but as the 'tough soft drink'. The advert was produced in two versions. One had a black cowboy shooting at several bottles, as on a range, and finding that Canada Dry deflected his bullets. The other had an American Indian having his tomahawk blunted by this brand after smashing the others. As the company told me, the idea was to encompass the diversity of communities, and the as-it-were 'red' Indian was adopted only after marketing tests had shown that there would be empathy and not offence from the Indo-Trinidadian community. So the drink is not a blank sheet upon which you can write anything. It has specific material qualities, such as black, and its own history, but these can be inflected in new ways.

I make the point below that commodities are in some respects better than categories of people at objectifying values. This seems to be a case in point. It is not that more Indians actually drink red sweet drinks and Africans black sweet drinks. In many respects the 'Indian' connoted by the red drink today reflects the Africans' more nostalgic image of how Indians used to be, or perhaps still should be, relating back to the era of the sugar industry. It may well be, therefore, that the appeal of the phrase 'a red and a roti' is actually more to Afro-Trinidadians, who are today avid consumers of roti. Meanwhile, segments of the Indian population have used their foreign education and local commercial success sometimes to trump the African population in their search for images of modernity, and thus readily claim an affinity with Coke. That is the nature of stereotypes. You can't physically consume another human being as African or Indian, but you can consume a drink that has connotations of ethnicity. This is important since, in truth, no Trinidadian is really just one or the other. Both Indian and African roots penetrate deeply into what Trinidad has become, so every Trini of African origins has many Indian aspects, including a fondness for a red and a roti, while Trinis of South Asian origin share the Carnival and calypso culture of Africans. The simplistic discourse of ethnic identity makes people out as belonging to one or other group, while being able to drink either a red or a black sweet drink comes closer to the actual hybridity of contemporary Trinidadian identity.

None of this would have been evident if we had merely accepted the idea that, by consuming Coca-Cola, Trinidadians were acquiescing in their colonisation by US cultural imperialism and losing their cultural specificity. Actually, we have reached precisely the opposite conclusion: that, ironically, it is Coke itself which has the capacity to adapt to this very specific and nuanced sense of what it means to be a contemporary Trinidadian. At this point Coca-Cola really couldn't look more like a finch. I almost wish Darwin had come along to see such a curious-looking bird as the Trinidadian Coca-Cola.[6]

The drive to consumption[7]

The example of Coca-Cola suggests that Naipaul could not have been more wrong. Trinidad was about the most creative and dynamic place imaginable, and this was precisely because it was quintessentially a consumer society and not a producer society. One of the biggest clues, though I didn't understand it at first, came as soon as I started to meet people. In London, when first meeting someone, the standard question I used to ask was 'And what do you do?', assuming that a stranger's first point of identification came from their work. One's labour is the source of one's value. But in Trinidad I quickly realised that this question caused confusion, even offence. As time went by I began to understand why. Work was generally regarded by most lower-income Trinis as simply something one had to do to earn a living. This was not from choice, but from necessity. It seemed therefore obvious that no one would choose work as central to their own sense of who they really were. That would be demeaning. This attitude might go all the way back to slavery and indentured labour, though that is mere speculation. Instead Trinidadians would light up as soon as the conversation turned to things that they chose for themselves, which might be music or clothing, relationships or cars, sports or drinking, or indeed the entire gamut of modern consumption. For them it seemed obvious that it is these consumer activities that generate and express personal authenticity, in stark contrast to labour.

As happened time and again, I started to appreciate that there was a 'logic' to Trinidadian concepts that merely exposed the illogical nature of my own presumptions – one of the great joys of being an anthropologist. Why should one privilege the wage labour that someone else makes you do over the acts of consumption that one chooses for oneself? Furthermore, on what basis was consumption assumed to be less creative than production? Working in a factory or growing sugar cane are not especially creative acts. So, far from being a pale imitation of other places, as implied by Naipaul's *The Mimic Men*, everything in Trinidad seemed to be wonderfully...well, Trini. In sports they played cricket, but the atmosphere of cricket bore no relation to the same game played in the UK, and there were local versions of sports, such as windball cricket or small goal football. The creativity of music and dance was particularly engaging, but actually Trinidadian Hinduism also seemed different from my experiences of religion in India.[8] The same applied to the weekly newspapers, not to mention the food or the way people shopped.

The way in which different facets of consumer culture in Trinidad seem to form a more coherent logic was described in more detail in the book *Stuff*,[9] and requires a brief summary here. The starting point was an observation about the particular place in which I was living – Montrose, on the outskirts of Naipaul's birthplace of Chaguanas. I undertook a survey of local business and found the main industry in this area was dominated by three huge firms, all devoted to car upholstery. In the recession period, when I started fieldwork, upholstery was becoming restricted to repairs to vehicles such as taxis. But the industry had arisen during the oil boom, when apparently most new cars had their first outing to these upholsterers. There they would be given a makeover involving everything from the dashboard to the boot, with designs such as fake snakeskin or a black leatherette streaked bluish and silver, marketed under the title of 'New York by night'.

It wasn't just the upholstery of the car that had become so expressive. In Chaguanas, car ownership had been quite rare before the oil boom, and yet it was clear than in a short time cars had become much more integral to life here than in the UK. I soon discovered when I took my daughter to nursery that people stayed in the car right up to the time it was their turn to reach the nursery doorstep or remained in the car at the edge of the park while their kids played. I soon learnt that individuals were located more often through the car parked in front of a house than their house number. The local press constantly spread scandal and innuendo through reference to car ownership, as in 'The leader has a nickname which resembles that of a popular large local fruit, and he drives a taxi which is neither too dark nor too light', or talked of an AIDS victim 'whose husband drives a Mazda'.[10] The retailers I studied, irrespective of what they were selling, routinely decided their expectations of a particular customer entering their shop on the basis of their car. So I would be told that a Laurel driver bought this product but a Cressida driver would not buy that.

Most people memorised a whole raft of car number plates, which became central to local gossip, as everyone soon knew that a certain car had been seen outside a certain house. Car parts were also much used in sexual innuendo, such as a mistress being referred to as a 'spare tyre', and the lyrics of calypsos, where girls who picked their men by the bodies of their cars rather than those of their drivers were called 'gasbrains'. Where I lived people seemed obsessed with car upkeep. One neighbour washed his car at least once a day – twice if it had rained – with particular attention being paid to the area within the treads of the tyres. I have seen men's faces crease with tension because someone (probably me) had slammed their car door.

Further observation had shown that there was a clear division between shops devoted to the car interior and the car exterior. The latter included the tinting of window glass, the adding of stripes to the exterior body, or the sale of wheel hubs, a key fashion item, which at the time was shifting from metallic to white. I then realised that these activities seemed focused upon two distinct groups of customers. While a car with fake tigerskin and pink plush interior might also have flashing lights on the exterior, in general retailers distinguished between 'a cool look' emanating from stripes and tinting and 'the flash look' embodied in some of the more outrageous upholstery.

The presence of this upholstery led to an investigation of other sites in which similar materials could be found. One conspicuous consumer on the same high street turned out to be the funeral parlour, where coffins and the more expensive and luxurious caskets were almost invariably lined with deep buttoned upholstery. A much more widespread use was in the living room interiors, where plush carpets and maroon three-piece suites were becoming de rigueur. Some of these were covered in clear plastic sheets, making them rather uncomfortable and sweaty to sit on, but preserving the upholstery. This could also be found on car seats.

Following the textiles then led to a reconsideration of the home interior, which was a major part of my fieldwork, including a systematic analysis of some 128 living rooms.[11] This involved the analysis of the sofas, the wall decorations, the artificial flowers and, more generally, the use of layers and covers, which ranged from crochet-style toilet roll covers to stuffed toys in plastic bags. The degree of repetition and order in the decoration of home interiors showed how this aesthetic reflected certain core Trinidadian values. These practices of covering and layering were associated primarily with the family, with education (filling up the person with qualifications) and with building long-term futures.

At this point, the fact that car accessories were sold by two distinct types of shop, dealing with interiors and exteriors respectively, could be related to the contrast between the two major festivals that dominate Trinidadian cultural life: Carnival and Christmas. Christmas was clearly the festival of the interior and the family. The months before Christmas are devoted to cleaning the home and buying new furnishings and replacements. The following days see a process of centripetal sociality, during which relatives, friends and even work colleagues (who visit at no other time in the year) will come by to the house and eat some black cake and drink some ponche de crème.

The symbolism of Christmas as the inward-facing festival of the domestic is directly opposed to Carnival as the outward-facing festival of the street, with its rowdy disorder of public display. Where Christmas should be celebrated in traditional style and continuity with the past, Carnival is a festival of the present. Even if you parade in the same costume as the previous year, you should

make the costume anew. Carnival is based around a long tradition
of symbolic inversion. It starts with a night-time festivity that
speaks to the ideal of things, usually hidden, which become
revealed by the dawn. It retains strong connotations of freedom
and emancipation and has deep roots in the particular history of
Trinidad and slavery.

All of which leads us to a still wider analysis of cosmology in
Trinidad. The book which provides the detailed descriptions
and analysis was called *Modernity: An Ethnographic Approach*,
because ultimately I argued that what starts with car interiors and
exteriors ends up as a thesis about time itself. I theorised that
Trinidad is a peculiarly modern place, partly because, torn from
Africa and India in the searing rupture of slavery and indentured
labour, it lacks local roots and traditions. The result was a dual
aspiration: on the one hand, an enormous concern to embody
freedom, to refuse the shackles of custom by remaining transient
and of the moment, but equally the opposite desire to establish
new historical roots and localised identity through building the
long term. The opposition between these two relationships to time
itself was expressed here in festivals but also in everyday consumer
culture, such as car interiors.

But why was the place I lived in dominated by car upholstery?
The majority of people in this area were of South Asian origin,
and the male Indians are the dominant car-owning group. It
appeared that the car had become a key expression of their emulation of a sense of freedom often associated with the lifestyle of
Afro-Trinidadian males, but constrained by modes of family life
and attitudes to possessions associated with Indo-Trinidadians.
The car is a substantial possession which usually 'delivers' on its
promise of greater autonomy and freedom, but this does not necessarily mean that the driver abandons one set of values for
another. The transference of domestic upholstery to the car seemed
to be directed at retaining Indo-Trinidadian values asserted in the
world of the domestic interior, while enjoying experiences which
in Trinidad are often seen as in direct opposition to these values.
As is often the case, material culture becomes an attempt to keep
'the best of both worlds' in response to contradictory values.

This conclusion rests on an association between consumer
goods and generalised categories of people, which raises another
issue. It was quite clear in Trinidad that these distinctions in values

I had found through the analysis of cars, living rooms, coffins, clothing and the like could also be expressed as a dualism based on stereotypes about people. I would commonly be told that men – in general – were only interested in the present and the exterior, while women in – general – were orientated to the long term and the interior. Young people were said to be present orientated, while older people looked to longer-term projects. Black descendants from Africa could also be labelled as only interested in today, while it was claimed those with ancestors from South Asia cared more for family and the long term. It didn't matter that I could demonstrate again and again that these generalisations might be wrong. Actually, I knew many Indian women who were far more expressive of Carnival values than black men. But the stereotypes remained. So a typical academic analysis would conclude that consumer goods were being used to express, reinforce and reproduce these same stereotypes.

My observations from Trinidad complicate this picture. To my mind, the key point is that Trinidadians, as other people, possess a certain logic of cultural value which exists through a process I would call objectification. We see our values reflected back in the order of all the things around us. But for this purpose human beings can be made into very useful objects. These stereotypes are based not so much on actual people as on the use of generic categories of people, which are then used to express and illustrate core values, such as feckless transience or devotion to the future of the family. My sense was that, as consumer culture grew rapidly following the oil boom, it was material objects such as cars that were increasingly used to express those same values. If anything, cars work rather better than people if you are aiming for some sort of expressive logic. You can separate out car interiors and exteriors as being catered for by different shops to show more clearly this opposition in values, for which reason it seemed to me that, the more consumer culture grew in Trinidad, the more values and the logic of cosmology were objectified in material things rather than thorough categories of people. In which case, consumer culture didn't necessarily reinforce such stereotypes. Instead it is possible that objects took over something of this burden as the idiom of objectification. As people used metaphors based on consumer goods, they were less dependent upon race and gender, though ethnic stereotyping was otherwise being reinforced by politics. I readily admit that the suggestion that an increase in consumer culture might lead to a diminishing of prejudice may seem outrageous to many and is quite hard to demonstrate. But my job is to follow the logic of evidence and analysis wherever it leads me, and I think this is worth exploring further.

The point of this analysis is that I hope it justifies the very term *consumer culture*. A consumer society is a society that is saturated with consumer goods. But this analysis suggests more than merely the presence of those goods. It shows how quickly it is goods such as cars, foods and gifts become the principal idiom for expressing core values. In this section I have described what we may call Trinidadian cosmology, which is characterised better as a systematic opposition between opposed beliefs than as a single belief system. But it was easier to see these as a systematic and underlying order through studying the pattern of commodities than by simply asking people about their values. As cosmology, it is as much an example of culture as would be the study of canoes, cows and ritual objects in classic anthropology. It also suggests something else. As promised, my analysis directly refutes Naipaul's *The Mimic Men*. The car may have spread recently and rapidly as a result of the oil boom, but the picture I have painted does not suggest at all that Trinis were merely mimicking the car cultures of other societies. This extensive car upholstery business seemed to have become a very Trini business, expressing local oppositions and concerns.

It is as though a whole new vehicle was created in Trinidad that brings mobility not just to persons but to cosmology itself.

Is consumption capitalist?[12]

The final argument in my book on modernity rests on the ambiguity of the verb 'to forge'. On the one hand, forgery sounds like Naipaul's mimicry, a term describing inauthentic fakery. On the other hand, forging a sword is an example of our most romantic medieval expression of authenticity. In Trinidad consumer culture, we seem to weld together both aspects, the forge and forgery – literally in the case of steel band, perhaps the best-known example of a cultural form that was invented in Trinidad, and this time exported from there to the rest of the world. I started this chapter by noting that about the only thing Trinidad actually produces is oil, which results in a hell of a lot of surplus oil drums. But Trinidadians don't just leave these drums to litter their landscape. They consume them in an act of creative production. When I go and hear a classical concert in Trinidad – Bach or Wagner performed by an orchestra of seventy musicians, all playing varieties of steel drum, from bass to tenor – I still marvel at the sounds that have emerged from this act of forgery. But, I put it to you, which kind of forgery is this – the authentic medieval blacksmith or the fake? I would say both, and that's the point.

So the examples of cars and Coca-Cola are to show how consumption becomes an aspect of culture. They are not intended as claims that these goods are good or bad. I am not saying that making something more Trini is necessarily positive. If Trinidadians appropriate drug culture, with its associated gun culture and gang culture, and they make these very, very Trini (I suspect they do), I can't see why that would make drugs, guns and gangs any better. So the aim is not to legitimate but to understand how culture works today. But, having done this through attention to ethnographic details, I also want to make explicit the consequences for our theories of consumer culture more generally.

The fieldwork in Trinidad wasn't just in repudiation of Naipaul's suggestion that the island had lost its culture. The problem also stemmed from my original understanding of culture from the reading of Marx. As I have noted, it was Marx above all who privileged the proletariat and manual labour and critiqued the capitalist system as the exploitation of that labour. By contrast, Marx had very little to say about consumption. Into that vacuum academics have poured themselves tales of what they think Marx should have said, almost always resting their case on one key assumption. It is taken for granted that, to the degree to which it is the creation of capitalism, consumer culture is also an expression of capitalism. So, for example, the culture theorist Baudrillard[13] established his reputation by arguing that it was consumption rather than production that most fully expressed capitalism today, and most cultural criticism from the 1970s onwards seems to concur.

However, just as Coca-Cola may not express global homogenisation, I think we also need to step back a moment and consider the relationship between capitalism and consumer culture more generally. As noted in the preface, egalitarian Norway and the highly individualist US are both among the world's wealthiest societies and are clearly consumer societies. True, the vast array of things that people buy in London are produced by some variant of the market or capitalism. So it is not surprising that we see the shopper as the end point of that system. For the likes of Baudrillard, people are merely the mannequins who wear the clothes which ensure that the fashion system can continue to perpetuate its drive to constant profitability. But, whenever I go with an actual shopper down an actual high street, I see something very different from this assumed passivity. Shopping is the topic of the next chapter, but, as a preview, let us imagine that a friend goes to a shopping mall with the express aim of buying a new dress, maybe one with a print to complement the less colourful items they already possess. In the first shop there are eighteen print dresses, but for one reason or another none of them quite work for this friend. She continues down the mall to visit eight more shops with between seven and twenty-four possibilities in each. But at the end of the day, having inspected more than 150 possible print dresses, what does she do? She goes home without buying a thing because the shops didn't have the right one for her.

What emerges from this little scene is that the shopper has a quite extraordinarily precise idea of themselves in relation to the vast array of consumer goods. Despite the huge amount of money clothing companies have laid out, weaving their commercial webs in order to entrap this little insect, they have failed to find anything sufficiently seductive. When we pause to think about it, this is rather extraordinary. After all, what's so special about this friend? Probably nothing at all. I am certainly not trying to suggest for one moment that she is engaged in some kind of heroic act of resistance to commercial culture or capitalism. She wants to buy their dresses. Her problem was not that commerce provided so many different print dresses, it was the very opposite – that they still didn't manage to produce 'her' print dress. The more dresses they produce, the more her rejection confirms her own specificity.

All those dresses, on all those hangers, in all those shops, do seem quite an overwhelming, even alienating mass that we have to contend with. But just suppose my friend had finally bought a dress – on the next shopping expedition, she probably did. Once the purchase was complete and the dress was matched with shoes and jacket and accessorised and taken out to the pub, it would no longer be a sign of that initial shop environment, those rows and rows of clothing. At this point it would most certainly be her dress. She might well become instantly protective. No her sister absolutely cannot borrow *her* dress. She would be mortified to see someone else at the pub wearing the same dress. Suddenly this dress is a clear signal of her specific taste, personality and presence in the world. Any consumer object in a shop is technically alienable – i.e., free for anyone to buy as long as they have the money. But a dress once purchased and possessed immediately becomes the very opposite, something inalienable, that cannot be purchased or even borrowed by your sister – she can go and buy her own bloody dress.

From completely alienable to completely inalienable doesn't sound like continuity, but rather like contradiction. And that – I would like to suggest – is precisely the point. It's not just that academics write about capitalism as alienating and reducing us to mere mechanisms to secure its profits. I think we, the customers, have pretty much the same feelings about it. Capitalism quite clearly is alienating. Markets are so vast that most of the time we don't even know where the thing was made or how it was made. It is just an item that appears in a shop, and our response to this is to become still more pernickety as a means of establishing our retained sense of personhood in the light of the threat of being reduced merely to the passive consumer.

My point becomes clearer if we were to imagine an alternative situation. Let us say we lived in a communist state, where goods were produced by state factories without any market mechanism. Would the situation be any different? I would suggest not in the least bit. People who lived in communist countries, such as the former Yugoslavia, had an even stronger feeling about the way shopping needed to be an expression of what was often a desperate attempt to assert themselves against the alienating aura of the state as the provider of those goods.[14] The Marxists were correct to see capitalism as intrinsically alienating; they just did not predict that communism would be too. In the end the woman in the ideal sharing community, such as the kibbutz in Israel, never could be reconciled when she saw a woman she didn't even like wearing a dress she had once made, but which had been redistributed to someone else in the name of ideology. Within the UK we have the same issues with state-provided goods as we do with market-provided goods. The state provision of childbirth facilities also seems alienating, redolent of the anonymity and white coats we associate with modern science. So people form alternative movements, as in education or the NCT (National Childbirth Trust), which expectant mothers use to humanise the process of childbirth, which we strongly contend should feel that much more human, rather than being the passive recipients of modern science and state provision.

What I take from the Hegelian theory, which lies behind much of my work, is an argument that consumption and consumer society do not express or continue the processes that lead up to them. Instead, they form what I would term a dialectical point of negation. What this means is that we recognise that we live in the world in which forces such as markets, states and science, which give us tremendous advantages, also have huge costs. For example, most of us fully recognise that it is absolutely right that we should live in a state characterised by a powerful bureaucracy that treats us anonymously, because to treat us personally would lead to corruption. This anonymity is the price we pay for believing in scrupulous fairness through which we are all treated the same. Similarly, markets seem highly effective ways of distributing goods, but there is nothing intrinsically positive about them. If we allow them to act without regulation, they have a natural tendency towards exploiting people for the sake of profit. Science is the third foundation of the modern world, the source of a much increased and healthier life and of the extraordinary capacities of these consumer goods. But it can just as readily make atomic weapons and pollute the planet as save it.

These are the necessary contradictions of the modern world; the positive and negative consequences are two sides of the same coins. But we don't just accept such contradictions, we try and confront the more negative consequences. Consumer culture is the point at which we confront one of these problematic consequences, which is the sense of alienation we feel as a result of the vast scale and scope of the market, the state and science. One of the ways we keep our anonymity and distance is through the use of money. Instead of dealing personally with these forces, we transact with them and protect our persons through money, which keeps them at arm's length. But it is the same anonymity which protects us from corruption that makes us also feel depersonalised and alienated. Once we have used money to purchase consumer goods, these become our possessions and the source of a very different kind of production and creativity. We work on these possessions and sometimes make them very personal and expressive of our specific values and relationships. This is what makes them part of the process we call culture, so that 'consumer culture' is not a contradiction in terms. As in Trinidad, consumer goods are increasingly the main form of expressive implement from which most people today create cultural life. But this is not simply an individual activity; it occurs mostly at the larger level of society and the way in which a society understands and expresses itself, in areas ranging from the media and the high street to fashion. Consumption is not just an individual process of choice and self-expression. That is why I have deliberately placed this chapter, which takes the entire island of Trinidad as its example, before a chapter on shopping, which is orientated more to the behaviour of individuals. I am an anthropologist emphasising these wider social transformations rather than a psychologist. One of the reasons I think Trinidadians prefer to be known for what they do as consumers, rather than being associated with the work that they do for wages, is that they recognise that consumption, not labour, is the primary point for their creation of an inalienable life. For them, labour is not the ultimate source of value; consumption is a far more appropriate foundation, because it is less oppressive. So this is what I meant earlier when I stated that, in theoretical terms, consumption can become the negation of the alienability associated with the market, the state, science and, indeed, labour.

So Baudrillard could not have been more wrong.[15] No one wants to feel like a passive mannequin, hence all our invective and diatribes against corporations. Everyone had a soft spot for Google and Apple when they started out as the underdogs of commerce. For those old enough to remember, this was true even of Microsoft when it first started. Bill Gates was then the common man in his Gap jersey. But, once these companies become big enough, in our heads they turn into 'corporations'. And then the resentment and feeling of oppression begins. We seem to have a natural tendency to resist, resent and then negate anything that becomes sufficiently abstract or distant by reason of size – as we should. However, if this is true of the abstract scale of capitalism, states and science that need to be tamed, then there is another candidate. I think it should be true of the abstractions of academics and theories as well, which also have a tendency to become oppressively esoteric and obfuscating. As I argued in *Stuff*, anthropologists should avoid trying to become philosophers. To me, that's a demotion, not a promotion. So, since this last section seems to be heading in the direction of a general theory of inalienability, this may be exactly the right point to go back to Trinidad and pay a visit. Let's see if we can ground these abstract ideas in something more concrete. Actually this is a particularly good time to visit Trinidad – I can see they are gearing up to celebrate Christmas.

Whose side is Santa Claus on?[16]

There are many Trinidadian songs with titles such as 'Trini Christmas is the best', and I find it hard to disagree. I can't play a musical instrument to save my life, but I retain a hazy memory of one year joining a band. One Trini friend played Afro-comb against cheese grater, I played bottle and spoon, and another friend used a leaf as a trumpet. We went from house to house happily accepting a slice of Christmas black cake from each, but more importantly a shot of ponche de crème, made from condensed milk, spices, raw egg and overproof rum, until we finally collapsed in a stupor, I know not where. OK, the snow may be fake and sprayed on but, by the same token, the sunshine is real.

I guess I was not that surprised to find that behind all this lies an accusation that is entirely familiar from the UK. Once upon a time Christmas was an authentic festival, redolent of true religious and social values, but today it has been thoroughly corrupted and rendered inauthentic by consumer culture and relentless materialism. A typical diatribe from a local Trini newspaper is entitled 'Deck the malls'. It notes: 'What a paradox! To find a bit of Yuletide festivity one must visit bastions of capitalism – the mecca of modern day shopping – the malls...they have now become little centres of Yuletide charm...what with its myriad decorations, festive piped music, weekend activities such as choral singing and parang, and of course we still buy, buy, buy.'[17]

They are not exaggerating. Many retailers noted that December sales for certain products, such as curtains, exceed those of other months by up to a factor of eight. They joke about how they could be closed for the rest of the year with little loss of profits. In the town of Chaguanas, where I lived, people set up stalls in front of the shops a few weeks before Christmas, and by Christmas itself there were stalls in front of those stalls, so you could hardly walk in the street. The papers were full of 'letters to Santa', where children wrote about which computer game they were expecting to receive this year. All of this was contrasted with lashings of nostalgia about the old days, when people would boil up the ham in an old pitch oil tin and when Christmas was the direct expression of family warmth and proper values.

This is a worldwide complaint. As several academics have noted, Santa Claus became an established figure largely through the promotion of US commercial popular culture, including Coca-Cola advertisements. As such, he seems not just to replace the centrality of the Christian figure of Jesus but to invert the symbolism. Whereas Jesus is young, thin, ascetic, serious and from the Middle East, Santa Claus is old, fat, jolly and from the North Pole.[18] Christmas seems generally established as *the* festival of shopping, such that, instead of being able to pause, enjoy and gain a sense of the festival, it seems compulsory to labour in sweaty, overcrowded shops to finish buying the requisite useless gifts for all and sundry. Once it was authentic; now it is tawdry.

In Trinidad the labour is a little different. As noted above, Christmas is the festival of the home interior. People spend weeks taking out all the furniture, cleaning, tidying and putting it back. Then on Christmas Eve they seem to do the whole thing all over again, but even more frenetically – not to mention all the preparation of food and drink. Unlike in the UK, the main emphasis on purchasing is gifts not for people, but for the home itself. Not only that, but, if during the year you took advantage of a trip abroad to buy a new item for the kitchen or living room, it is often stored away and brought out and placed in position for the first time only on Christmas Eve. Most important are the curtains. If you have the money, you may well buy new ones; if you don't, then you will have the old ones cleaned. Often after midnight, when everything is prepared, these curtains are hung up. Then finally one goes to bed, as the house is ready to play host to a huge

Christmas family lunch the next day and all the visiting of neighbours, friends and kin on the following days.

Christmas even has its own ethnicity in Trinidad. People from all three main religions – Hindus, Muslims and Christians – celebrate Christmas, Divali and Eid as national festivals. But Christmas is specifically the *Spanish* festival with *parang* music (whose lyrics are in Spanish) and Spanish foods such as *pastelle* and *ariapes*. Hardly anyone speaks Spanish, but then the term 'Spanish' doesn't actually mean 'from Spain'. It has come to stand both for the ancient past of Trinidad, including the indigenous population that mixed with the first Spanish colonists, and as shorthand for 'mixed origin'. A person whose actual ancestry is a mixture of South Asian, Chinese, French and African thereby becomes 'kind of' Spanish. It seems that Christmas is a festival that thereby transcends ethnic difference and comes to stand for the land. The Hindu figure of the Di, or the spirit of the land, has Spanish features.

Yet, if Christmas has this highly positive value in objectifying the sense of being Trinidadian, this has not emerged through some official or government sanction. There is no clear intention behind any of it. There is absolutely no individualism to this act of consumption as cultural appropriation. It arose entirely out of the dynamics of popular culture, including the consumer culture of music, food and drinks. Once again, it is the material culture of consumption that seems to succeed as an instrument of creative authenticity, suggesting that perhaps we need to look a little more carefully at the association between Christmas and materialism. If you survey the gifts that come out at Christmas, they are not actually all fripperies. Mostly they are items for the home, or clothes that people would have had to buy at some time or other. As we have seen, many of them were bought on other occasions and just stored until Christmas. In earlier times it was customary to take new purchases, such as a car or new toys, to church and have them especially blessed at Christmas. All of this suggests that perhaps what we have here is not the secularisation of materialism, but the very opposite, an attempt at the sacralisation of consumption.

Just as I argued previously, in more abstract terms, so I would argue more concretely for Christmas. People are well aware of the potentially alienating nature of consumer culture. If an individual Trini just goes to a shop and buys a new fan for their home, nothing has been created in terms of social relations. This is simply an abstract purchase between two people, who don't know each other, kept at a suitable distance through the neutral medium of money. But if that same fan is purchased as part of the refurbishment of the home – which is expected at Christmas – then it becomes integral to a festival, which is more effective than any alternative at expressing a deep sense of family intimacy and close social relations. This is the festival which first bonds family, then wider acquaintances such as work colleagues, through the home, and finally, as the Spanish festival, effectively comes to express the solidarity and commonality of Trinidad itself, transcending the divisions that plague it the rest of the year. By associating as many of the annual purchases as possible with this festival, the potentially alienating and abstract relation to the market is replaced by the inalienability of re-establishing core values and core social relationships. Christmas may be deeply associated with materialism, not because it is an expression of materialism, but rather because it has been recast as a festival for the suppression of the antisocial aspects of modern materialism.

This argument applies to more than just Trinidad. Historians have noted that the key moment in which the modern Christmas was resurrected from what had become a relatively neglected event was through the inspiration of Charles Dickens. Still today, the one story that is most commonly associated with this festival is Dickens's tale *A Christmas Carol*. The direction of this foundational 'myth' is from Scrooge, who represents the sheer abstraction of money as mere base coin without human or social qualities, to Cratchit, who understands that money has to be turned into an instrument for the creation of human values and the warmth of the family within the home. The means for this conversion is Christmas itself. So, at just that historical moment when capitalism is coming into its ascendency, Dickens is creating a new festival whose primary achievement is to tame the antisocial tendencies of capitalism's movements towards mere abstract capital, a story about how to bring base money back to its 'proper' role in the service of humanity. It neatly expresses the core opposition between what anthropologists call the commodity economy and the gift economy.

So the idea that Christmas has entirely lost its origins in religion as it sold out to consumption needs some revision. In both Trinidad and Britain, Christmas finds ways of linking back to the transcendent. When I was a child in London, the key ritual of Christmas was watching the queen's TV broadcast. The celebration by the individual family around the Christmas table had become the microcosm that was taken up by the (then rather less tarnished) image of the royal family. This, in turn, led Christians back to the origins of the festival in a divine family scene around a crèche. If Christmas has become a means by which we try and tame the antisocial nature of the commodity, this doesn't seem so out of kilter with its origins in religion as this ritualised worship of the family.

Conclusion

Consumption has many consequences. In the final chapter we will address climate change, but first I want to establish both just what it means to become a consumer society and its consequences for that population. I used the case of Trinidad, since the shift to mass consumption, following the oil boom, was more recent and more dramatic than that in most other places. It might be thought that the aim of this chapter has been to conduct a defence of consumer culture. That would be half true. There has been an entirely consistent theme, an insistence that consumer culture is indeed culture. This was in opposition to the dominant arguments that dismiss consumption as a loss of culture, where culture is defined as that condition of authenticity that existed in earlier times. I argue this with some feeling, precisely because I am an anthropologist. Anthropology is the discipline most associated with this dominant argument. The classic *New Yorker* cartoon with the caption 'Put away the radios, the anthropologists are coming' suggests that modern consumer culture was used as the very definition or boundary of what anthropologists would not study, because consumer culture was not regarded as culture on a par with that of tribal or village societies that were taken as untainted. My concern is not just with anthropologists, but that we have used anthropology to represent this ideal of authenticity more generally.

This chapter has not just argued that consumer culture should be regarded as authentic, it has also rejected the assumption that it is necessarily individualistic, materialistic, competitive or, indeed, capitalist. The analysis has been of Trinidadian cosmology as expressed in the logic of material culture and Christmas as an anti-individualistic and anti-materialist festival. The chapter has been much more about consensus than about competition, and I would expect that these arguments would have been equally applicable if goods had emerged from a communist system of production. The sheer scale of such a communist state and its centralised distribution of goods would still be massive and alienating. So a consumer culture is not just culture, it is culture as we know it, entirely amenable to the same kind of anthropological study as any tribal or village society. I have used the case study of Trinidad, but I believe this to be generally true. To that extent, this is indeed a defence of consumer society. But, as noted with the earlier example of gun and gang culture, it does not follow that the specific content of a given consumer culture is good or bad with respect to the welfare of that population. The argument has been that this is culture, the idiom by which we become and subsequently understand who we are. This chapter is not an argument that consumer culture is necessarily beneficial. What we call culture is commonly a process that demands conformity, conservatism and, indeed, oppression. Culture being normative is in many respects inherently illiberal, although it may strive to be consensual. So merely showing the ways in which Trinidad constructs itself as a consumer culture is to imply that Trinis are, in that respect, the same as people anywhere else, neither better nor worse. What Trinis don't seem to share is our assumption that it must be labour rather than consumption which is the true source of authenticity. So, if you go to Trinidad, best not start with 'and what do you do?'

3

Why We Shop

When I started researching consumption, at first I avoided the topic of shopping. The reason was that in my theoretical writings I had made the point that, if we reduced consumption to shopping, we would then ignore what to me was a more important process. For me, consumption was not just buying things, it was the way we subsequently transformed the goods that we had purchased – a much more active process. Also the topic of shopping seemed to focus on individuals, while I see consumption as more of a social process, which shifts goods from alienable into inalienable. In anthropology we believe it is better to work within a society other than your own, since otherwise you take too much for granted as simply the natural or obvious way of doing things. Nevertheless, after working on consumption more generally in Trinidad, I felt it was then more possible both to work on shopping and to research in London without these dangers. In this chapter, I summarise the results of that research in three sections. The first two are theories of shopping, which are also concerned with its more immediate consequences for the family and for individuals. In the third section I tackle the wider ethics and consequences of shopping.

A first theory of shopping – peanut butter[1]

Susan was not particularly looking forward to going shopping. She was taking not only her own two children, but also two of her brother's seven children, who had been staying with her, not to mention an anthropologist. The older children would have preferred the more prestigious West End of London, but settled for the large shopping complex around nearby Wood Green. The trip would be dominated by Susan's self-appointed task of buying clothes for her sixteen-year-old niece Joanna. Susan had decided that she might be best placed to intervene between various competing interests. Susan's mother had recently complained that Joanna's clothes were either too 'ethnic' or too revealing (short skirts or see-through items). Susan could see trouble ahead, as they were all going to be together for a family holiday in Italy. She feared that Italian men might be more predatory than English men. On the other hand, she wasn't particularly conservative, and there was little point buying clothing Joanna didn't like and then certainly wouldn't wear. For her part, Joanna was not especially clothes conscious for a sixteen-year-old girl. To come shopping she wore a short, black, fairly unpretentious dress.

The combination of having to mediate self-consciously between her relatives, the fact that she didn't see herself as having any particular flair for fashion, and the constant demands of her own small children all meant that Susan started off with some trepidation. Nevertheless, her approach to the problem was skilled and effective. She came up with the idea of bicycling shorts (this was 1995) as sufficiently fashionable and sexy to please her niece, while from her point of view they were safer than a short summer dress or skirt. The top proved more of a problem. We were looking for a white blouse, but these seemed to vary between those found in teenage shops, which were too much like crop tops, to the rather dowdy blouses found in older women's shops. We found a blouse with 'tails', intended to be knotted together at the front, which looked suitable for a holiday, but the material was poor quality and the size was wrong. We considered several others, including one with shoulder pads, but rejected them on various grounds. After half a dozen more shops we found another shirt designed to be knotted around the midriff, made of better material, the right size and in the sale. Although she did not particularly like the buttons on the sleeves, Joanna was as happy with this as Susan. This looked like a success. It certainly would be if it helped prevent some of the tensions that threatened to erupt around various relatives' concerns with the effect of a sixteen-year-old's sexuality on a family holiday in Italy. Joanna seemed pretty easy going, but then she wasn't with her own nuclear family, and therefore was perhaps less concerned to use shopping as a chance to assert her growing autonomy as a teenager.

This was pretty much the only success. Susan purchased a card for her own tenth wedding anniversary that was to be celebrated the next day. She found most of the cards utterly tasteless, but in the end settled for one of two cows nuzzling with pink mouths that had been made to look like hearts. She noted that the formal present for a tenth anniversary should be something made of pewter, but she and her husband could not think of anything of pewter they wanted. Last year they had bought a coffee grinder, something that seemed a luxury in comparison with their current spending, as they were saving against the envisaged costs of moving house. This time they might buy some china. In general, Susan noted that her husband was not very good at celebrating such events, although she tried to reconcile herself to this on the grounds that 'that is typical of men'. In a more ideal world, shopping for both card and present would have been celebratory, but then in that world her husband would have been doing the buying. Given his failure to exploit a potentially romantic occasion, her buying of both card and gift seemed to have been reduced to an empty gesture, fulfilling the obligation to do the proper thing.

Susan also had a plan, based on earlier shopping trips, to make the whole thing more attractive by having lunch at McDonald's. This would be the treat to compensate to her toddler for having to spend the day shopping. But the toddler in question fell asleep in the buggy at just the wrong time and so missed this intended highlight. Her older son was interested in a competition being run by Coca-Cola, but since the token that told you whether you had won was inside the folded lid of the cup, he spilt the drink four times on his clothes while trying to look for it. Similarly, Susan was sensitive to her nephew's boredom from having had to spend so much time looking for clothes for his sister, and she determined to get something for him as well. But she found that, at thirteen, he was too small to fit anything from the men's shops, while he rejected the idea of clothes at the children's shops, and by this stage she was too tired to do other than admit defeat and hope she could buy him something another day. His sister was none too happy with him, since they had decided to buy a card for Susan and her husband, but he had forgotten to keep this a secret from Susan.

The biggest failure of the expedition was yet to come. Before we started out, Susan's three-year-old had claimed that he enjoyed shopping, and Susan encourages him to start having his own taste and choices. So when an opportunity arose at the supermarket she asked him to select something to eat. But by this time he was far too bored. He simply said 'yes' to a whole row of things in a manner that clearly showed he didn't really mean it. Frustrated by this, Susan took the last of his selections (some fish fillets) and bought them, choosing thereby to ignore the fact that they both knew he didn't really want them. Still, she said, 'I hope you will like it now you have chosen it', to which he replied that he doesn't like shopping with her since she always buys food he doesn't like. Susan responded, 'There isn't much you do like, is there?', and at this point the child flung himself in tears on the shop floor. Another problem arose in that the cat also needed feeding, and, as Susan noted, the cat is the most fussy eater of all, but she really couldn't be bothered with the queues at Sainsbury's (a large supermarket) just to buy cat food, and so settled for a different cat food, in what she herself probably regarded as a victory of hope over experience. Finally, in order to keep her own children happy, she spent some time in a toy shop, allowing them to run around and try things out. She didn't actually want to buy anything, but felt some token purchase was needed in order to compensate the shop for her having, in effect, used it as an entertainment zone, but then she couldn't find anything cheap enough to count as the token purchase she had in mind.

There are books around with titles such as *Why We Shop*,[2] but if you read them you will find they tell you nothing of the kind. They are actually about *how* we shop, because they are written to appeal to those who work in retailing and want ideas that will help them to sell more effectively. Despite the vast importance of shopping, there is really very little in the academic literature that even starts to answer plausibly this question of why we shop, in the sense of why we select the very particular items we choose to buy. Most of these more commercially minded books assume that research on shopping should take place in shops. Certainly you need to spend some time in shops, as in the little expedition just related. But mostly, if you want to understand why people shop, the place to be is inside their homes. The home is where the overwhelming bulk of commodities will be cooked in kitchens, hung in wardrobes, given to others. The second problem with conventional research is the assumption that you can study why people shop mainly by asking them. Much of the data derive from questionnaires and focus groups. However, language often does not provide a reflective analysis of why we do something; it is a justification rather than an explanation.

Reflecting upon Susan and her shopping expedition, our first observation is that this is a million miles from the kind of moralising discussion of shopping one tends to encounter in journalism. If you knew about shopping only from newspapers, or indeed from the way we commonly discuss it, you would have to assume that modern shopping is essentially individualistic, hedonistic and materialistic. Yet who actually accounts for the vast bulk of everyday shopping? Susan is entirely typical in that, although she works, she also regards herself as a housewife. While in our society a minority of consumers might appropriately be described as individualist, hedonistic and materialistic, the least likely candidate for this would surely be a housewife. Susan spent the entire day shopping, but the only time she buys something for herself is to enable her husband to give her a present he won't otherwise get around to buying. She really couldn't be more selfless. As for hedonistic, the best Susan could hope for was that the shopping wouldn't be quite as dreadful as she feared. Could she be materialistic? Does she really need these things? Every single purchase was required to satisfy and to fit a niche in the lives of others for whom she felt concerned. Finally, none of this seems, at least at face value, to be some kind of passive response to the pressures of commerce. Even the McDonald's fiasco came about primarily from her use of their competitions and marketing for her own purpose of compensating family members for having come shopping in the first place.

To try and answer the question of why people shop, I spent one year on a single street in North London, shopping with the people who lived there, and spending still more time in their homes. I was accompanied by my then PhD student, Alison Clarke,[3] who was concentrating on more informal modes of provisioning, such as second-hand goods and the use of catalogues. The example of

Susan is taken from this collaborative project. I prefer to under-take research in London through locating a random street, where I cannot predict who will be present within those walls, and then carrying out research with whoever lives there.[4] This is in direct repudiation of the ways in which social science is usually con-ducted, by selecting people as the target of research in terms of given categories such as ethnicity, gender or class. A problem with conventional research is that, if one conducts a project based on selecting people in relation to, for example, class, then it will hardly be surprising if the resultant report reveals that – guess what? – class is important.

I am not suggesting for a moment that these social parameters are not significant; they may end up being the fundamental core. But I think the argument is much more convincing if I start by not making assumptions as to which will matter to my analysis, and let these emerge so strongly from my fieldwork that I can't deny them. This was very much the case with regard to shopping and gender in the North London study. In the end, almost everything I was to say about shopping was saturated with issues of gender. But I myself found this all the more convincing because I had tried hard not to look for gender as integral to this project. My method, like all successful ethnography, was not to have a method, but to remain sensitive to what worked best for that particular project. For example, I found that people in a London street don't like you knocking on their front doors, even when it has been agreed you will check each day to see if they are going shopping. I learnt to sit in my car in the street and phone them, then wait ten minutes so they could freshen up, put down the loo seat, or whatever; only then would I go and knock on the door.

Most of our everyday shopping consists of groceries and cloth-ing, with less common excursions for buying presents or some-thing needed in the house. Much of our shopping revolves around household relationships, and one of the problems with simply asking people why they shop is that some of these household relationships are difficult to talk about. The maternal ambivalence of a mother, who experiences severe restrictions on her life after having children, may finally have led Susan to buy the fish fillets she knew her child didn't really want. A housewife may resent the fact that her husband really could shop for his own trousers, but, even if he finally agrees to do so, he may just go off and buy the first pair he sees, which is really not going to help him get the promotion the household needs. So she might as well just buy the trousers for him. Thus it may well be the unspoken aspects of relationships that are the key to determining why people buy what they buy.

In *Stuff* I presented a theory of relationships based on a study of the mobile phone. But this theory first emerged from my earlier study of shopping, in which I called it my 'peanut-butter' theory. It is a theory derived from many encounters with mothers such as Susan, faced with dilemmas such as what to buy for their children. The attraction of peanut butter is that it is generally regarded as reasonably healthy – at least compared to much of the junk food that children seem to demand if given free choice over what they buy for themselves. Yet at the same time it is something most kids like to eat, and accept as evidence that you are paying attention to their desires.

To generalise from this, let's say there are two aspects to every relationship. The first is what you think the other person should be like as an example of the category they represent. Everyone has pretty strong feelings on what a mother, a lover or a brother should be. So, using the more technical term, this can be called the *normative* aspect. It's not just descriptive, there is an implied moral adjudication of what sort of person they ought to be. However, at the same time there is everything you know about how that individual person actually is. Not *a* wife, but *your* wife; not *a* brother, but *your* actual brother. So my theory states that most purchases are designed to diminish the discrepancy between these two states – the normative and the actual. Peanut butter is both something children should eat and something your particular child does eat, so it works.

One way of seeing this is to watch how mothers shift their pattern of purchasing according to the age of their children.[5] At first the child is without autonomy. We can happily project onto them whatever we desire for them to be, dress them in faux-peasant lacy wear representing some kind of primitive innocence or an idealised version of ourselves. We can relive the best of our own childhood, waiting impatiently to read them our own favourite children's books or play with a particular toy we loved at their age. Then, as we start to meet resistance and refusals, we compromise. OK, so they have the sweet tooth of their father or start to be fussy about what they wear, just like their mother. We may accommodate and decide we really do like Disney films after all. A mother has two children, one of whom is said to be like a 'dustbin', eating just about anything, and the other being extremely fastidious and abstemious. After a while it becomes obvious that the two represent her own internal ambivalence in relation to food. After reading about Susan, one can see why parents in our study so much preferred to shop for their children without the presence of an actual child. It is so much easier to spend ages getting the right food item or clothing for the idealised object of one's love, as compared to when the children are actually there, embarrassing you in public with their greed and materialism and their less than ideal behaviour.

So one's attitude is relative to one's expectations and norms. Eleana may be happy that her husband shows no interest in buying clothes, since this confirms her norm as to what real men are like. Real men are simply not interested in clothes. But Anna would be deeply upset by that same man, because for her a real man buys his own clothes and doesn't expect her to do it for him. Similarly, Eleana may depend upon her husband to supply the household with 'treats', while Anna may be resentful that he buys only the treats, leaving her with shopping as a chore. In an ethnography of a town in northern England, Simpson[6] notes how divorced women may bitterly resent money spent by their ex-husbands on expensive gifts for their children when they visit their father, because he wants to compensate for his absence. As the mother, she lacks the funds to do the same, and would prefer that money to come to her in maintenance payments. Both are aware that shopping shifts and creates normativity as well as reflecting it. If they let this become the pattern of their relationship, it will become an expectation and acceptable norm.[7]

Watching new couples shopping in a supermarket, one can observe their tentative gestures in selecting an item, as they seek for congruence and confirmation as to which areas they will bond through sameness, and which through difference. It's OK that they both love fish and chips, or it's just fine that he likes only pizzas and she only pastas, as long as they can agree that sameness or difference is respectively attractive. The classic failed shopping is when men buy sexy lingerie as Christmas presents for their wives, only to see it returned to the shop the week after Christmas, as the actual partner refutes the projected norm of what men think a woman should be like and should want.

For this theory to work, we have to watch how shopping helps resolve these discrepancies between the normative and the actual, but we also need some ideas as to where the normative comes from in the first place. We might consult various academic writings about gender in our society, or simply listen in to the way in which the people we study talk about such matters. During the shopping research a very useful point of reference turned out to be hanging out in the local hairdressers, overhearing conversations, but it could have been a pub or any number of social situations. For example, when listening in to women in mothers' groups, or neighbours on a housing estate, the singularity of their particular spouse becomes secondary to referring to him as an exemplification of the category husband. More of the conversation was about what 'husbands' are like, rather than any particular husband. In fact, the point of comparison was more often a character in that week's television soap opera. Men's conversations in the absence of women, for example in the pub, similarly tend to the generic and stereotypical, though with rather less reference to 'wives' and rather more to 'women' and what women are like. A popular misrepresentation takes us to be individuals desperately trying to create our individuality in the teeth of sanctioned norms and constraints. My evidence was very much in the opposite direction. People were buying goods to help another individual better conform to their general sense of what people within that category are supposed to be like, rather than fostering individual creativity or difference. The emphasis is on those standard purchases such as yet more pasta dishes, little black dresses, or seaside holidays. This is not because of commercial pressure, but because of the attraction of norms themselves. This point is central to the following chapter on why people wear blue jeans.

The essential argument of the peanut-butter theory is particularly clear when we see these expectations projected by the shopper onto the intended recipient. Take, for example, shopping for pets (sort of persons). With pets, people are free to project qualities onto the recipients, who have limited capacity to tell you that they are not at all the way they are being represented. So you might think we would represent our pets as compliant and straightforward. Quite the contrary: pets are typically viewed as being difficult and obstinate. Cats, in particular, are seen as highly fastidious. For example, one owner noted that her cat demanded a specific ritual by which she would not eat at the time the food was put out, but only when she returned, and then only if it could see that the food was from a new tin. So lots of food had to be thrown out. A dog dominated household shopping, since he wouldn't eat ordinary dog food, only hard to find home-cooked pig's and chicken's hearts. A demanding pet is projected as 'full of character' and endearing, but more importantly as valuing the tremendous efforts of their owners to care for them. I have lived in many countries where pet cats and dogs exist, apparently happily, without ever receiving more than scraps from the table, mainly stale rice. You can't blame the pets. What we see here is really the ability of owners to convince themselves that the pet really appreciates this labour of shopping – in stark contrast to other household members. In such instances one can see how it is the shopping that constructs the pet as a 'proper' normative example of what a pet should be – something a little harder to do when it comes to husbands.

A much more serious but profound example comes from a study by the anthropologist Layne[8] on the anthropology and material culture of pregnancy loss.[9] Layne examines the complex means by which the developing foetus is constructed socially. One of the main instruments for helping an expectant mother envisage her foetus as a living being is through making it the object of shopping and the gifting of goods, something that echoes the most foundational theory of anthropology – the idea that society is created through exchange. As a result, a woman who suffers a miscarriage or stillbirth may continue with this same process, finding ways of including the child whom they would have had in gift exchanges, such as Christmas or 'would-have-been' birthdays. This may comprise buying gifts for it and, more importantly, giving gifts 'from' it to its siblings. So, in this case, the commodity, far from detracting from our humanity, is the main mode by which the mother can insist that what she has tragically lost is a person and not merely a thing.

If our peanut-butter theory is based on the discrepancy between a projected ideal and an actual person, then there is no reason at all why it shouldn't apply equally well to shopping for oneself. I recall many, many hours spent shoe shopping with Carla. Carla possessed four pairs of shoes and two pairs of boots. Leaving her job to study for an MA, and the subsequent need to dress down like a student, led to her initial formulation of the expedition as the need for 'sensible shoes that can be used in everyday settings'. I have elsewhere described the sixteen different pairs she tried on over one particular three-hour expedition.[10] The point is how her inability to like any of the shoes that accords with this formulation confirms her sense of herself as actually quite frivolous and therefore not really like a student is supposed, in her mind, to be. Indeed, she does ultimately buy sensible shoes, but several days later realises they are not 'comfortable', and returns to the high-heeled dressy shoes that are paradoxically more comfortable – at least in the sense that she has returned to what she takes to be her real self. Not everyone is like Carla. We can easily imagine another woman, less confident in her present image, who would leap at the chance offered by this change in their life to rethink themselves within this new normative model. So this tension between the normative and the actual works just as well in considering the contradictions within an individual as within a household.

This amounts to a theory of shopping, an answer to this question of why we choose any particular item of purchase, which now appears to be its perceived ability to resolve these tensions. But, as is often the case, the answer to one question begs another. The peanut-butter theory depends on a concept of normativity. The question where norms come from becomes tantamount to a general study of the culture of the time. This is too big a task for present purposes, but, rather than ignore the question altogether, I propose to give at least one example, which keeps us within the realm of shopping because it looks at the way the shops themselves can become pretty good at expressing such norms. Specifically, I propose to look at the relationship between shops and class. Anyone living in Britain soon gleans a whole sheaf of expectations about other people based on their identification with class. Once upon a time class may have been a relatively clear-cut distinction, with people unambiguously members of their distinct class group, which were opposed as clusters of taste in the manner described by Bourdieu in his book *Distinction*.[11] But one of the findings of this study of shopping in London is that most people are now so familiar with the spectrum of class in the UK that they are actually capable of seeing themselves in terms of more than one class.

This became evident because some of the people in our study shopped in two different North London shopping areas, Brent Cross and Wood Green.[12] Much shopping in Britain has become rather drearily homogeneous, with the same outlets, such as Boots, Marks and Spencer and W.H. Smith, more or less wherever you go. But there are a few shops at the extremes which seem to be able to grant these centres a particular class ambience. For those going to Brent Cross, this role is taken by the department store John Lewis, while for Wood Green high street it was a series of end-of-lease shops called 'cheap jacks', as well as the local street market, neither of which would have looked at home in the likes of Brent Cross shopping mall. The very same shoppers seemed to change their behaviour, sometimes even their accents, when shopping in each respective centre. Brent Cross found them more subdued, almost reverential, discussing functional aspects of clothing or kitchen implements as the voices of reason. In Wood Green they seemed to relax and take on a slightly more boisterous and personal manner, engaging in banter and spending more time being entertained by the very experience of shopping. If I had met them only in Brent Cross, I would have sworn they were middle class, if at Wood Green, then working class. But by now they have watched plenty of TV, which delights in portraying the quintessence of such class behaviour. So, without even realising it, they have become very capable at what is technically called 'code switching' between the mannerisms of each class.

What are the cues that tell shoppers which class they currently inhabit? In chapter 5 we will have reason to have another look at John Lewis and its relation to the concept of value, but suffice it to say that value at John Lewis is always a reasonable compromise between factors such as price and quality. Since the store saves you the time and trouble of working out this equation for yourself, it is an eminently sensible place to shop. It may not be the most glamorous of choices, but it is the least likely to represent a mistake. There is a powerful sense of trust that is really quite unusual in the world of retailing. People fully accept the John Lewis promise, that the same goods cannot be found cheaper at other shops. Everything is clearly categorised and in exactly the place it should be; all those miscellaneous haberdasheries and things that you really need can be found there. Assistants seem discrete, but knowledgeable and helpful, and facilitate the sense that shopping is all about making this right choice. It resonates with the very concept of 'middle' class as a reasonable compromise that is neither too high nor too low, but some sensible and suburban compromise within the field of class itself. It helps that John Lewis now owns Waitrose, the most evidently middle-class grocery in the UK.

By contrast, you can tell a Wood Green 'cheap jack' because goods are piled up on the cheapest of shelving units without any obvious logic. Prices are written in felt-tip pen on stars cut from yellow or pink neon card. Near the entrance is a very large bloke who would serve well as a club bouncer. Somehow you just know you are going to find there those plastic photographic frames, small electrical goods, glass ornaments, artificial flowers and a variety of temporary goods ranging from sweets to stockings. The shop will have a name such as 'Buy Direct', 'Elite Superstores' or 'Clearance Depot'. More than likely the man at the door will be black, the cashier will be Asian and the people piling up the goods will be white. Nothing is ever said to that effect, but somehow in the atmosphere of the shop you can just feel that conspiratorial wink that suggests that all this stuff came 'off the back of a lorry' or through some other vaguely illegal channel, which is how come it's so cheap. This is not so much a place to buy things as a kind of slightly illicit collusion between you and the shop to get things sold beneath the radar. I could tell you that, on systematic inspection, the same goods are often cheaper in more formal shops, but that would spoil the party. Between the feeling that you never know what other odd things might be on the next shelf and the unconstrained shouting of instructions between people at opposite ends of the shop, this is a shop with atmosphere. Perhaps it is the way it contrasts with the sameness of most corporate shopping, but a surprising number of people I went shopping with somehow felt that no expedition to Brent Cross was complete unless they also went to John Lewis and no trip to Wood Green was complete unless they also dropped in on a cheap jack. As so often with normative values, these are best created through systematic opposition: rational and legitimate order as opposed to playful and slightly illegitimate disorder. So the objective world out there seems to make the experience of class almost a part of nature – something we take as for granted as the landscape, along with gender and age. It also suggests that people enjoy partaking in and even performing class as culture, just as they see it happening on the television. The world of consumer culture helps thereby to objectify the norms that represent one side of this equation.

This is the essence of the peanut-butter theory. That other person is not just anyone; he is Robert, but Robert is also a representative of the normative expectations we would have of a middle-class young male cousin. Shopping is an attempt to diminish the distance between the person for whom one is shopping (which is often oneself), as an expression of the normative, and the actual person. You buy the only pair of jeans that you think a husband should wear and that your actual husband will wear, and then cook yourself a dinner that is the compromise between the sensible diet you should be on and the cravings you feel. You could leave the study of the normative in contemporary British society to sociology and the study of the particularity of individuals to psychology. But my argument is that all the interesting stuff lies in the tension between these two, and, speaking as an anthropologist, that is just exactly where I would like us to be in order to understand what is going on and why.

A second theory of shopping – sacrifice[13]

It's pretty common to talk about shopping and sacrifice – the peanut-butter theory alluded to the self-sacrifice of housewives. However, when I tell you that I am about to construct a theory of shopping based on the ritual of sacrifice, this is not what I mean to imply. I am not referring to self-sacrificial housewives, but to the precise structure of those ancient rituals of sacrifice studied by anthropologists. I mean standing at the point where some poor animal is having its throat cut, an activity which most housewives are only too happy to leave to professionals these days, but which I have had to witness many times. Theories of sacrifice are central to anthropology, partly because most societies seem to have been at some stage or other involved in rites of sacrifice, suggesting that these are foundational not just to religion but to the constitution of society itself. Although some contemporary societies still practise sacrifice, much of the literature is based on well-documented historical examples, such as those of ancient Greece. Within anthropology, the best-known general text dealing with sacrifice

was written by Hubert and Mauss in 1898.[14] More recent influ-
ential texts include Detienne on ancient Greece, de Heusch on
West Africa and Valeri on Hawaii. The early books of the Bible
contain endless and precise details of what exactly should be
sacrificed and how. Reading Deuteronomy or Leviticus reveals
sacrifice to be a routine aspect of life in ancient Israel, though
this could lead up to huge 'blow-out' sacrifices. Try imagining
the slaughter of 220,000 oxen and 120,000 sheep at the dedication of Solomon's temple (1 Kings 8:63); OK, now try not imagining it.

In the first chapter of this book, Grace noted the centrality of
sacrifice to any theory of consumption more generally, because
sacrifice is commonly the ritual that takes place at the moment of
transition between production and consumption. By acknowledging and propitiating the divine force behind creation, sacrifice
absolves us from the sense of guilt that we are in fact consuming
– that is, diminishing the world – and violence is a common theme.
The definition of sacrifice is that the offering is actually destroyed
– i.e., consumed rather than merely given. Following Hubert and
Mauss and most subsequent writers, there seem to be three main
stages common to many of these rites. The first is a vision of
excess. In the second, the actual burning of the sacrifice divides it
into two parts; one part is the smoke, 'the sweet savour' that
spirals upwards to become the food of the divine. In the third
stage the remainder of the sacrifice, which has now been sanctified,
is often consumed in a meal by the officiates. The way the meat
is distributed and the structure of the meal is often used to reflect
and thus sanctify the social order – for example, the special status
of the priesthood. The rite is also important in the way it establishes a connection between humanity and the divine, so that
gradually those involved approach a status in which they are fit
to commune with the divine; they then return, sometimes in stages,
to the more normal profane status.

In truth, this does not at first sound a whole lot like shopping
at a supermarket. For this comparison to work, even as an analogy,
I would have to demonstrate that shopping somehow turns expenditure into a devotional ritual that both affirms and constitutes
some transcendent force, which can then be used in turn to
sacralise social orders. But, yes, that's pretty much exactly what I
intend to do. The first stage of sacrifice centres on establishing it

as an act of violence – the potential destructive consumption of something – which is going to be negated in the second stage, tamed by its relationship to the divine.

When I started my fieldwork on shopping, before even observing any shopping, the first thing I tended to encounter was a discourse about shopping – that is, the things people said in general about it. Typically, my informants would make some remark such as 'You don't want to study me. Let me introduce you to my aunt – she is a *real* shopper', or make jokes about some celebrity addicted to shopping. Or I would be told that I should come back just before Christmas or for the January sales. In short, when I said I wanted to study shopping, people generally couldn't at first accept that this referred to everyday, ordinary shopping. The concept – shopping – is rarely initially a reference to the everyday acts of provisioning a household. Rather, it creates in their minds a spectacular scene of conspicuous consumption, by a highly dedicated shopper, at some cathedral to shopping such as a mall. It is also important that these individuals are almost invariably assumed to be women, sort of out-of-control women, blowing the household budget with some exuberance. So shopping as a concept seems to invoke something between a thrill and a fear. The same women, who otherwise are responsible for carefully looking after the resources of the household, will reappear suddenly as figures who wipe out the savings in an excess of desire satiated only through shopping. That, curiously, was seen to be the 'real' shopping that I was expected to study. The same discourse is reflected in journalism, where the favoured news items about shopping tend to be not about mundane shopping, but about the shopaholics, where shopping becomes a kind of pathology that needs to be cured. The word 'shopping' according to this view implies an act of destruction.

But I always persevered and explained patiently that, no, I didn't want to study their infamous aunt, I just wanted to study them and the mundane, boring shopping that has to take place day by day. Once this goal was achieved and we got down to the business of tackling the local shops, what was striking was not simply that what people actually do is different from this discourse, but the way in which it became the systematic negation of its own discourse. In other words, what I found was that, when they shop, people turn from an orientation that is all about

spending money to one that is all about saving money. By the time
they return to the house this process is complete, in that almost
all conversation is now about how much money they saved, where
it was saved and how they saved it.

Fortunately there turn out to be a multitude of ways through
which a shopper can represent and legitimate their actions as a
strategy of saving, quite apart from the direct issue of price. You
can buy a large quantity of the food, because that works out
cheaper per unit, or a small quantity, since that avoids waste. You
can tell me this furniture was amazingly cheap or that you bought
it on eBay. But also you can inform me that – of course – you only
ever buy furniture at Harrods, because then you know it will be
made of high-quality materials that last for ever, and so ultimately
this works out cheaper than the tawdry stuff I seem to buy for
myself. I think I can spare you further examples. I prefer to assume
that anyone reading this can immediately recall being bored silly
over dinner or in a pub by someone going on and on about all
the clever ways they saved money when shopping. And isn't it
irritating that so often they feel they have to imply not just their
brilliance in this art of thrift but that we, by contrast, are exceed-
ingly stupid because we ended up paying much more for the same
thing somewhere else. But then, let's be fair, are you really going
to pretend that you have never committed this very same crime?

One reason for this emphasis on saving is simply that it is true.
I would often compare the list of what people intended to buy,
written before we went out shopping, with the things that they
eventually brought home. One of the most surprising results was
the lack of evidence for any impact of advertising or other forms
of promotion. Children did refer to things they had seen on television and specific advertisements, but adults almost never do, and
the impact of advertising on adult shopping appears on the evidence of my research to be negligible. By contrast, it is actually
quite rare for a shopper to be unaffected by some claim that the
goods in question are on sale; either that the clothing shop has a
sale on that week, or an item of fruit is on a two-for-one offer or
is strongly discounted at that moment of time. Today it's almost
impossible to imagine a supermarket shelf without some of the
products having conspicuous labels telling you how much you will
save by buying them, often in greater quantity than you had
intended. Meanwhile, going to 'the sales' at the appropriate

season, such as January, has become something of a national habit, at least in the UK. Again you are made to feel that you are missing out if you don't go to the sales.

These two observations about the discourse and the practice of shopping could be considered on their own, but they make much more sense when considered together. The initial discourse is dominated by the vision of excessive expenditure, while the practice is dominated by the evidence of the subsequent savings. Both exaggerate, but the key point is that one systematically negates the other. It is as though the discourse sets up a fear of what might happen if consumption were uncontrolled, and then the practice takes every possible measure to ensure that this does not in fact happen – that consumption is turned into something quite different, something that is far less redolent of destruction and violence. The instrument that is used to negate that fear is thrift. But why thrift, exactly?

Thrift is what ensures that the household retains as many of its resources as possible when engaged in consumption. Since the time of Aristotle it has been taken as the fundamental virtue of the household. In many societies, one of the primary purposes of life is measured in terms of one's economic impact on the household.[15] In many villages in South Asia and South America, the criterion of a successful life is that by its end the household has increased in land and other resources, with life being seen as a failure if the household has been diminished during that period. In such societies this is both explicit and seen as central to the idea of value. A North London household doesn't look a whole lot like a peasant village. We tend to think rather more in terms of individual ambition and career. We also have many more single-person households, who are often quite transient in their occupation of a house. But, as I observed shopping more closely, I began to realise that we still have one trick up our collective sleeves that helps us to turn even this modern London household into something a bit more like traditional peasant houses. The action which acts to make thrift work effectively turned out to be the *treat*.

You could easily miss the treat, because quite often it was the very last thing a person picked off the shelf at the supermarket before they went to check out their baskets. One shouldn't overgeneralise, but a treat tends to be either slightly more expensive than it should be, somewhat more personal, or fattening. All right, it's not just you, even I am thinking – *chocolate*. Will it be Cadbury's Dairy Milk, less expensive but more fattening, or Green and Black's cherry, vaguely ethical and less fattening but definitely more expensive? Actually there are plenty of alternatives to chocolate. As I write, I recall one of my participants buying a bottle of something that they 'sort of shouldn't have', or an item of underwear they couldn't really say they 'needed', however much they stretched that concept. You won't be amazed that, for me, a treat also tends to be a book, especially that category of book I possibly won't read but feel I should have on the shelf.

Why do we buy treats? Sometimes it's just a little reward. We have spent an hour going through the list and tracking down every last object that the house needs over the next few days, and it seems reasonable to give ourselves a little something to show our appreciation for the labour involved in shopping itself. After all, if *we* don't acknowledge all that work, it's more than likely that no one else will. It can also be an act of compensation – when we feel depressed or disregarded, when that person failed to turn up or to mention that they love us, when it's just that no one has time to listen or they pretended to listen but turned away when we were talking and we felt humiliated. Then, even if we haven't been shopping, we might just feel the need to go and buy that treat anyway. The treat is simply an act of self-regard, something we buy for ourselves, a little indulgence, a comfort food – nothing huge, just something that says that, even if no one else cares for us or about us, at least we haven't been entirely forgotten. In the end we can always acknowledge ourselves.

Analytically, though, the treat does rather more work. If this is an act which is unequivocally about buying something for ourselves, then it suggests that the rest of the shopping was for other people. Everything else we bought was not a treat; it was an act of labour on behalf of the household. Paired with thrift, it helps turn the rest of that shopping expedition into something done for others. The treat is of particular interest when the shopper in question lives on their own, because it turns out that a single person is just as likely to buy themselves a treat as anyone else. This has the effect of dividing their shopping into two components. They might live by themselves, but still the bulk of shopping consists of simply the provisioning of their household – in this instance a one-person household, but still a household. By contrast, the treat is for them as a specific individual. That single person may be just as concerned with thrift as anyone else. A little of what we buy, the treat, reflects our individualism, hedonism and the rest of it, but it helps confirm that the remainder of what we buy is, like thrift itself, orientated towards some larger goal – in which case we are not entirely removed from the sensibility of the peasant household.

If you were to ask a shopper what precisely they are saving towards, what will happen to the money they have not spent, it is quite rare that they would be able to come up with anything specific. In general it is not that they are saving for this car or that computer. Mostly they are just practising the assumed virtue of thrift itself. This allows us to identify thrift with the second stage of the sacrificial ritual: that which acknowledges in sacrifice some divine or transcendent other to whom the smoke of the sacrifice ascends, while in shopping it is a generic sense of serving a wider generic purpose and not merely oneself. At this point we have not just negated the discourse of pure destruction in consumption, we have ensured that, prior to any act of consumption, we have first propitiated the bigger transcendent forces that lie outside our immediate concerns. We have done this by saving on behalf of that larger household as something we have a duty towards. Saving money is simply a kind of generic ethic: instead of being destructive, we have been good. A secular shopper does not need a concept of God to see this as being virtuous; they just need to experience it as the negation of that act of destruction posed by the discourse of shopping – at which point the second stage of the sacrificial rite is complete. We have given up something to a higher cause or power.

At the third stage of sacrifice we turn around and stop facing upwards towards the divinity or household as the bigger transcendent concern in life. From this point we gradually come down to earth and our position in society. Traditionally this was accomplished through a sacrificial meal. This was not just any meal; because the food had been sacralised, it has the capacity to sanctify the relationships that are made evident by the meal itself. In most societies there are strict rules about who gets which bit of the sacrifice and in what order it is distributed. Not surprisingly, given these are religious acts, it is often the priestly caste that is first favoured and whose special nature is thereby affirmed. Gradually things make their way to the commoners. This same relationship between groups of people is reflected in the wider humility of humans with respect to the divine. There is a parallel to this in Hinduism. If one goes to a Hindu temple, then typically one will leave with a food known as *prasad*, which you then distribute to others. Conceptually, *prasad* represents the leftovers from the offerings that humanity has presented to the gods. Within Hinduism, a person's leftovers are polluted by their saliva, and it would be especially demeaning to consume them. But as mere human beings we are only too happy to be demeaned in relation to gods, and their leftovers are more than welcome.

So, in the final stage of sacrifice, the proper order of the world is re-established: the inferiority of human beings with respect to the gods, and the proper relationship between groups of people. Mere objects cannot achieve this, but objects that have been sanctified can. In shopping in London, the purchased goods come back to the household potentially as representations of the labour of the shopper, whose devotion to thrift gives them the capacity for sanctification. This is why, almost invariably, the housewives whom I accompanied shopping had a very clear idea of how the whole thing should end. The aspiration was that these supermarket goods will be consumed in a family meal with everyone sitting around the table, actually noticing what it is they are eating, and acknowledging the labour that went into shopping and cooking. Or that they go out as a family for the day and one person actually notices that another is wearing that new outfit they spent so much time choosing, and tells them how good they look in it.

I vividly recall that, when I asked women in households if either their husband or their children made specific requests for what they should buy when they went out shopping, the answer would tend to be something like 'I only wish they would'. Such a request is not seen as a burden but as a validation, a sign that the recipient actually cares about what you are going to buy. The failure is the family that refuses to have a sit-down meal, because they can't wait to consume their food on their own in front of the TV, and they probably wouldn't be able to tell you what it was they had just eaten. In such cases there is no sacrificial meal blessing the household as a family; the rite has failed as a rite. Even eating the treat doesn't really taste as good, though we may feel an even greater need for it. There are reasons chocolate sells so well.

This idea of shopping as a success or failure brings us to what may be the ultimate achievement of sacrifice itself as a ritual. Assume for the moment that we are secular and do not believe in the divine. From that position, sacrifice was not in fact an act that propitiated the deity; rather, it was an act that created the belief in the deity. If we have a god that is constantly demanding things from us, including an array of sacrifices and the very best of our produce, then all that pressure and demand makes that god seem that much more real. A demanding god is much more part of our lives than an abstract or liberal deity who requires little of us or gives us flexibility in response. So in a way the prime purpose of sacrifice is that it effectively creates its own object of devotion.

This is what links the theory of shopping as sacrifice with the earlier peanut-butter theory. Remember the point that making our pets choosy and particular about what food they will or will not consume is a very effective way of convincing ourselves that our pets really care, not about food, but about us, that our devotion to them matters. Shopping as sacrifice is not experienced as a religious rite, but it is saturated with the devotion we associate with love. We don't just do this from need and duty; it is a means for expressing devotion to those we deeply care about. Above all, what we are trying to elicit, if not actually to produce, is love itself. This is why my original title for this theory of shopping as sacrifice was *making love in supermarkets*. My argument is that, if you just ask them directly about love, people tend to be awkward and embarrassed, but if you understand that shopping is largely a technology for the expression of love, as was evident from the initial case of Susan, then it becomes one of the best ways of studying love in families.

It's hard to be good[16]

So far this presentation of shopping seems to imply a rather benign aspect to most people's intentions, with a focus on love and altruism. Actually I think that is correct, but it is also obviously an overgeneralisation, and to end this chapter I am going to argue, rather surprisingly, that even love and altruism may have a rather unexpected downside. In any case, even at an individual level, we can imagine that, delving through someone's basket of goods, we would find items other than love: envy, for example, certainly a good deal of self-interest, vanity and greed – perhaps even self-loathing, revenge and jealousy. The earring that is really rather a lot like hers, but obviously better quality; the CD with the musician who stole my girlfriend. I see these other issues as present, but rarely as dominant as love or routine. This is partly because the emphasis has been on the figure of the housewife, who commonly is the most altruistic of all members of a family. At this point we might also wonder if there is some way we can link this altruism with that which is of central concern to the first and last chapters of this book: the relationship between consumption and care for the planet and its population. Surely if shopping is more about love and altruism than we realised, then it should lend itself also to being green and altruistic with regard to the welfare of other people and the planet more generally. But the whole point of engaging in patient ethnography is to realise that things are often not quite as we might have predicted. It turns out that this altruism is not going to help as a foundation for saving the planet. Paradoxically, it turns out to be a major part of the problem.

One of the leitmotifs of both this book and its predecessor, *Stuff*, is that research that depends entirely upon language is highly suspect. What people say is more often a legitimation than an explanation for what they do. An example of this came through the shopping study, where I was interested in people's feelings about supermarkets and corner shops. By and large, when this was a simple survey question, most people seemed unequivocally in favour of corner shops and against supermarkets. Focus groups were more nuanced, but still could include a litany of praise for the preservation of the corner shop as against the supermarket. But working with people as individuals and talking in the privacy of their homes, with the full knowledge that they almost always shopped in supermarkets and hardly at all in corner shops, revealed quite the opposite. Most people in these contexts are actually extraordinarily positive about supermarkets and dislike or even detest corner shops. Part of the problem is that the reasons they dislike corner shops include issues such as racism, which they fully recognise as illegitimate. More generally, they have a keen sense that one is *supposed* to favour corner shops and to state otherwise would reflect badly on them. So, not surprisingly, this does not emerge from other methods of investigation such as questionnaires. Surveys and focus groups are much better at telling you what people think they should feel than what they actually feel.

The same issue is bound to apply to a topic such as ethical shopping. Since at the time of my work there was little by way of ethical alternatives in clothing, the term refers mainly to decisions to buy organic, fair-trade food or items such as free-range eggs. Most people are by now well aware of what they are supposed to feel and think about such issues. If my research had been limited to conversation, then I would have concluded that ethical shopping mattered considerably to the people on this street and that it constituted quite a high proportion of what they bought in the shops. One problem is that, even when there is evidence for such shopping, the grounds can be ambiguous. Shopping at charity shops may be a good example of altruism or may be just a way to save money. This was not a topic in my research, but work by others, such as Nicky Gregson, demonstrates that, for example, shopping at charity shops is driven overwhelmingly by other desires, such as hoping to pick up bargains or to find unusual goods, rather than a concern for the wider ethics represented by such shops.[17] Similarly, the act of buying organic food or non-farmed salmon can be evidence for a person's concern for the health and welfare of the planet, but equally just for the health and welfare of themselves, given the fear that added hormones and other substances might do nasty things to the eater. My evidence suggests that the attraction of organics lies in large measure in the way that they allow people to choose a product that they regard as healthy for themselves and their families, a largely selfish concern, but one that can be presented as an act showing concern for others such as the future of the planet.

As I looked more carefully at my evidence for what people actually buy, as against their conversation, it was clear that ethical shopping represented a far smaller proportion of actual purchases than might have been expected. This led to a further investigation as to why there should be such a marked discrepancy. In the end there seemed to be three main reasons which accounted for the lack of ethical shopping, at least for people on this street at that time. One seemed to be a kind of pervasive stereotyping of green people and activists, who seemed to be understood as almost an anachronism – ethical activities are just 'so eighties', or slightly strange and uncomfortable. The figure Linda Snell from the radio soap opera *The Archers* was seen as typical of someone whom you tried to avoid, lest they harangue you with their various good causes. The original health food restaurant in the UK was called Cranks, and there remains a general ambivalence about ethical activism as undoubtedly worthy, but not really as appealing as might have been expected.

The second reason could be extracted from careful listening to the way people talked about ethics within the general framework of how they tried to be good. In conversation a wide range of different issues tend to get bundled together. A concern for the developing world doesn't necessarily sit with a concern for the environment when it comes to buying goods from, say, East Africa and thinking about the airmiles involved. Supermarkets don't help, in that they use semantics to imply all sorts of concerns that are really more hints than actual evidence for ethical priorities. Is a 'fresh' egg an ethical egg? Words such as 'good' and 'healthy' and concern for the planet are now used so loosely as to become quite diluted in their impact and veracity – more an example of commercial *greenwashing*. But it's easy to blame commerce. Much of the conversation about ethics also concerned issues such as healthy eating and, above all, dieting. A core concern when shopping is to avoid bad foods such as those high in fat or cholesterol. The trouble is that all these things get discussed at once. So a person may talk about exploitation or pollution but end up feeling they have done their bit and been good because they purchased various diet and low-fat goods. Diet foods might be helpful to their waistline, but in truth are not going to be of any great consequences for either global exploitation or environmental sustainability.

Beyond both of these, however, lay a third explanation, which takes us right back to the two theories of shopping already proposed. It corresponds to what I will call, for present purposes, a contradiction between morality and ethics. In discussing the analogy between shopping and sacrifice, the concern that was found to dominate people's actual shopping, as opposed to merely talking about shopping, was thrift. It was evident that, if one had saved money and bought things in the sales, that represented the shopper as a moral individual concerned to keep resources for the future and shop wisely on behalf of their household. The priority here is clearly one's own family. By contrast, all forms of ethical shopping, whether organic or fair trade, were automatically assumed to be more expensive than buying regular goods. So the purchase of ethical commodities would be at the expense of thrift. The ethical concern for wider issues of the planet and other people was thereby, in practice, always seen to be at the expense of the moral concerns for one's own family and household. This then becomes combined with the first explanation. Moral concerns for one's own family are experienced as a kind of natural and warm attitude. Concerns for the planet and exploitation are focused on more distant and abstract goals, which don't carry the same sense of immediacy and warmth. This is why, paradoxically, the more ethical the activist, the more they become regarded as a cold rather than a warm figure – again Linda Snell of *The Archers* serves as an example. We all know we are supposed to support her, but the loveable and less ethical rogue is much more appealing. So, curiously, both the theories that were proposed earlier count now also as reasons why people do not engage in ethical shopping as much as we would like. The problem is not that people are hedonistic, individualistic and materialistic, but precisely the opposite. It is because they are thrifty and moral that they fail to be ethical. This is not the result we might have wanted, but please don't shoot the messenger. I am just studying these things, not causing them.

4

Why Denim?[1]

When I first started to conduct research on consumption, the intention was to have consumption acknowledged as an important process in its own right and not merely as the secondary outcome of production.[2] I wanted thereby to create an autonomous space where we could start to think about consumption in and of itself. In the past two chapters it has become evident that consumption is now a pivotal process in the lives of families and in the construction of wider orders, including the expression of our core values and beliefs about the world. So far this has been accomplished by an examination of consumption culture as a whole in Trinidad and the specific practice of shopping in London. In this chapter we complete the trilogy by focusing on just one consumer object – denim blue jeans – and one very simple question – why do so many people wear them? Once again, I will start by showing why this question cannot be reduced to the most immediate or obvious answers, such as its benefits to commerce. Instead we need to address what people understand by and intend in wearing jeans. But, as in the last two chapters, the consequences of wearing jeans will be shown to reach well beyond intentionality, and this is why we need anthropology and other academic tools to examine these questions and not merely reiterate the views of informants.

Denim blue jeans also provide a link between my previous book, *Stuff*, with its emphasis on material culture, and this second volume, which turns our attention towards consumption. The reason for studying blue jeans comes simply from their material ubiquity. They are a prime exemplification of what we can call the 'blindingly obvious', both as material culture and as consumption. The blindingly obvious is that which is so clearly in front of our noses that we do not pause to ask the obvious question as to why they are there. As such they perfectly illustrate what in *Stuff* I called the humility of things,[3] the way that objects frequently avoid drawing our attention but become the material background or canvas to everyday life. Because this is true of material culture, it is equally true of the consumption of material culture. To understand jeans we have to push ourselves out of the frame where we take them for granted, and instead stare at them as something incomprehensible.

The Global Denim Project

When I started my project on denim blue jeans, along with Sophie Woodward, I took advantage of the invitations I am fortunate to receive requesting lectures in various parts of the world. I would find some nondescript part of Seoul, Rio, Melbourne, Bucharest, Istanbul or Beijing, and just stand on some street and wait for exactly one hundred people to pass in front of me, counting how many of them were wearing blue jeans. Now, although I am not talking about global demography, since this would not be true of much of the rural populations of China and India, I feel able to say, as a result of this street-corner loitering and somewhat random sampling, that probably in most of the countries of the world today close to half of the people are wearing denim blue jeans on any given day – i.e. a typical figure in my notes would be around 50 per cent.

The term 'blindingly obvious' seems warranted by the degree to which we simply don't seem to be able to focus on what is in front of us. There is a vast academic literature on haute couture and journals with titles such as *Fashion Theory*, but it seems that, the less likely we are actually to wear something, the more attention it gets in journalism and academic writing. There are loads of articles about haute couture. By contrast, there is not a single paper in *Fashion Theory* about denim blue jeans, the single most common garment we actually wear.

So the next stage is to stop taking for granted the fact that we wear jeans so often and start seeing it as almost miraculous. Why on earth is this the case? The first point to make is that it surely puts the nail into the coffin of commercial causation. We have a terrible habit today of thinking that, because we live within what we used to call *capitalism*, but these days is usually termed *the market*, everything we see must be a result of capitalism or the market as cause. But let's think about blue jeans for a minute. Certainly pretty much all of our blue jeans are supplied through mechanisms that exist within capitalism: production, distribution and retail. However, this is the 'how', not the 'why', of blue jeans distribution.

For the market to be a cause, an additional argument would be required showing that getting people to wear blue jeans enhanced profitability and the interests of those in commerce, as compared to people wearing an alternative garment. It takes barely a minute to appreciate just how much the opposite is true. Commerce is desperate to promote fashion, the idea that we need to buy new clothes, because what we possess is no longer fashionable. Commerce wants us to wear things briefly and then buy others. Commerce wants us to buy more expensive designer or special clothing. But denim blue jeans are the most conservative and enduring of all clothing. The best-known brand of Levi's has pretty much always been the best-known brand. The basic denim jeans of faux-indigo cotton twill, with double stitching and rivets, are almost identical in markets from Laos to Turkey to Mexico. They have changed remarkably little in a hundred years. Despite pundits constantly claiming the death of denim, it simply pushes on relentlessly.

Furthermore, these are the garments we wear more often than any others. We keep them for longer in our cupboards, and we care less about the state they have got into, so we don't necessarily throw them away when they are dirty and worn. We may even think at that point that they have only started to get better. Clearly, commerce can make money from blue jeans, but it would make far more money if it could persuade us to stop wearing blue jeans altogether and buy other, more fashionable, less long-lasting clothes instead. I have interviewed individuals responsible for the jeans department in major clothing firms who were supposed to bring out a new collection of jeans each year. I actually ended up feeling a bit sorry for them.

Yes, of course I am aware that there exist designer jeans, styles such as boyfriend or 'skinny' brands of denim that cost hundreds of pounds per pair, but this is a very small part of the blue jeans market. For example, in the UK there has been a big increase in the sales of denim jeans in recent years. But this is mainly at the lowest end of the market, at places such as ASDA (Walmart) and Primark.[4] In our research in London, Sophie Woodward and I found that, while many young women possessed branded jeans, these were kept for special, the more dressy occasions. On a day-to-day basis people wore the most nondescript, cheap jeans and in many cases didn't even know what brand they were. So, once again, the study of commerce takes us only a very small way in our attempt to research and understand the specifics of consumption. There has to be something else going on here. Nor is it just jeans. Clothing shops are full of windows that scream 'Buy me: I am interesting, different and the fashion of the moment'. But travel on the underground train or look down the street and it is obvious that the dominant colour is drab – browns, blacks and greys, as though the colours and prints of the 1960s Austin Powers have leached down the plugholes. I once wrote a paper called 'The little black dress is the solution – but what's the problem?'.[5] It was in thinking about the little black dress that I first came to appreciate the role of anxiety in determining what we wear. So the issue is not restricted to denim blue jeans, but jeans do dominate, and for the purposes of this chapter I will keep them centre stage.

The first observation we made about blue jeans is that they are global and ubiquitous. The second comes from a study by Sophie Woodward, initially undertaken as a PhD under my supervision, which resulted in a book called *Why Women Wear What they Wear*.[6] For this project she reasoned that you could not understand women's relationship to clothes just by observing what they wear in the street. You needed to be present when they woke up in the morning and got dressed, because very commonly they would start with an aspiration to wear something more interesting and different, put the clothes on, look in the mirror, lose confidence and take them off again. I did not to enquire too closely into how she managed to conduct this fieldwork, but the point was that you learnt just as much from discovering what they rejected when they got up in the morning as from what you saw them wearing later on. Most important was the observation that, when they were feeling particularly anxious and unconfident about alternatives, denim emerged as a kind of default wardrobe position. You could always come back to denim.

So we have ubiquity and now anxiety to consider. But with denim blue jeans there is a third rather extraordinary aspect.[7] At least until recently, when some other genres of clothes have started getting into the act, there were no other items of clothing that we would find in our retail stores which appear to have been speckled with bleach, torn at the knee, stained with rust, worn out with rubbing, ripped and frayed in several places and subjected to a whole series of other destructive processes. If we saw signs of such abuse on any other clothing we possessed, let alone intended to buy, we would ourselves become pretty distressed. The nature of the denim twill helps create the fading effect but does not of itself explain why jeans, which for nearly a hundred years were sold without distressing, developed this unique other market. As it happens, I can relate the story from my own memory. As a teenager I hitch-hiked around free rock concerts, wearing flowered shirts and blue denim flares – jeans that were worn so much, in such rough conditions, and with so little attention to washing and care that after a while they became naturally abraded and frayed in just the manner that is simulated by commerce today. Those were the days when the only way one stopped wearing such jeans was when your mother or girlfriend burnt them.

My hazy recollection was that this was all about getting stoned. Not me, of course – the jeans. At some point commerce decided to imitate this process of abrasion by developing the practice of stone-washing, whose effect was to imitate the wear and tear of long-term usage. That was the start. Today we have an entire industry devoted to this process of artificial distressing. Apart from stone wash, one can opt for acid wash, moon wash, monkey wash, show wash, white wash and mud wash. Chemicals such as potassium permanganate are applied to shift the tinting. Resins may be used to set creases at particular places in the jeans. There is ozone fading or water jet fading. There are various forms of sandblasting or hand-sanding, either on a flat surface or on dummies. Typical special effects include whiskering, creating crease lines around the crotch with lasers or abrasive rods. If one wants really fancy results, a laser beam can be passed through a shaped mask that comprises an aperture of the desired shape, and is then deflected by a mirror to strike the textile substrate. Behind all this technology we have the absurd situation where workers in factories in Mexico or Turkey may find their lives shortened by working with dangerous chemicals, or suffering silicosis from sandblasting, so that we can buy clothes that save us the trouble of actually wearing them down ourselves.[8] We really are buying other people's lives etched into our trousers.

Distressing clearly developed in response to the extraordinarily personal relationship that people, such as myself, developed with their jeans. Jeans have become the most intimate garment we possess. Underwear may seem intimate, but it doesn't change over time to become associated with our specific individuality (well, mine doesn't). Some jeans sites discuss and promote this personalisation. They suggest that you don't wash your jeans for quite some time so that, when you finally do wash them, the creases that show up will reflect your own unique way of walking and working.[9] Commerce is here reflecting back the quality of individualising that gave rise to jeans distressing.

Now, when there is just one unique feature, interpretation can be a problem, but where we have three extraordinary traits that can be attributed to blue jeans we can perhaps start to relate them to each other. We have found that blue jeans are the most global garment in the world, but also, for many, they are the most intimate and personal garment we possess and the garment that seems best able to relieve us of anxiety in terms of our appearance in public. It would be a little unreasonable to regard this combination of traits as mere coincidence. A starting point might be to suggest that most of us today feel the need to claim a relationship to the larger world, which, through television and other exposure, appears to us as ever increasing in extent. We all want to feel we are citizens of that world. But the downside of this claimed cosmopolitanism is the sense of alienation given by the sheer scale of that world. We can claim to be part of this world, but that reduces us to a microcosm in a vast landscape, an insignificant particular. So how can we be global without losing our sense of our specific and individual personhood? Perhaps it helps if we can develop a garment that is simultaneously both the most global and the most personal thing we can wear. Perhaps putting on blue jeans helps in some small measure to resolve this contradiction of being able to encompass the world without losing ourselves in it. It helps if it also resolves other more personal anxieties about how we look to others. Perhaps when it comes to the phrase 'being in the world' we may not all read Sartre and Heidegger, but we can be comforted by wearing denim blue jeans, which do rather more to resolve our existential conflicts.

Once established as a global garment, denim is subject to all those processes of localisation that were discussed in the chapter on consumption in Trinidad. In order to respond to this combination of global and local factors, Sophie Woodward and I created something we called the Global Denim Project.[10] Given that we had no money or institutional backing, this consisted simply of our putting up a website with that title, but an advantage of the internet is that nobody can stop you claiming something on a website.[11] What we argued was that, in academia, most people choose something to research on the grounds that no one else is studying that topic. We thought, why not reverse that logic? On the website we declared that we would be working on denim for at least the next five years, so anyone who hadn't yet chosen their own topic of research might consider working on an aspect of denim. At least that way there would be other people to talk to, and academia could be a little more sociable. We were also curious to see if this kind of 'open-source' approach to academic study could work.

This strategy was surprisingly successful. By now there are over twenty projects, including those from people who heard about the site and decided either to associate research they were already doing with our site or to start new projects on denim in response. The publications that have resulted are clearly testimony to the localism of global denim. There are some great stories – for example, from the ghettos of Rio, where kids in the 'funk' movement adapt a specific form of Brazilian denim, first developed for the nouveau riche, which then become so well known that Brazilian jeans now have an international reputation based on the idea that something Brazilian is inherently sexy. My own project looked at why people were reluctant to wear jeans in the Southern Indian state of Kerala. Another project looked at how, as a US icon, jeans become used in new campaigns for recycling used clothing. Others looked at jeans in production, as in export processing zones in Egypt, market sellers in southern Brazil, or marketing through Bollywood stars. One project examined jeans among hip-hop youth in Germany, another the history of socialist Hungary. Jeans appear as the sexy link between a good fit and looking 'fit' in Milan and as part of kinship relationships within the Chinese family.[12] So each place has its own story and jeans their own local significance. These local analyses complement the more global perspective of our project.

One of the most important papers in these collections is by a historian, who challenges the usual stories of how jeans originally become popular in the US around the rebellious youth styles represented by film stars such as James Dean and Marlon Brando.[13] Instead, Comstock reveals a much more complex picture for both men's and women's relationship to jeans, in terms of the emergence of mass culture in the 1930s. Certainly history is important in understanding jeans.[14] It is remarkable how few people today even know that jeans are blue because indigo was one of the first dyes which did not require another material (a mordant) to help it affix as a dye to cloth, and as such was hugely important even during pre-history.[15] As Taussig[16] has pointed out, Haiti was originally colonised not for sugar plantations, but for the indigo plantations that were needed to dye the uniforms for Napoleon's vast armies. Similarly, under British colonialism, many of the fields of India were planted with indigo. But there is a difference between knowing the history of a thing and explaining why it continues to be significant and popular today. For example, it is clear that at one stage Americanisation was hugely important in the spread of blue jeans. Yet today the people I worked with in South India had no idea that jeans originated in the US, assuming they were either Indian or (mysteriously) German in origin.[17] So the current spread of jeans in this area cannot be an example of Americanisation or of youth rebellion. If we want to understand jeans today we need to study them though ethnography, as contemporary material culture. At the same time as developing the collaborative Global Denim Project, Sophie and I made the commitment that we would also study jeans through a more concentrated ethnographic-based project within London.[18]

How jeans became ordinary

For this purpose we used the same technique I had devised originally for the shopping research, taking randomly selected streets
and working with whoever happened to be living there. Initially,
we intended to work on the question of the relationship of jeans
to anxiety that I have just discussed, but as the study developed
we came to appreciate that even more important was the capacity
of jeans to objectify a state best understood as simply being *ordinary*. In our research we of course asked people about why they
wore jeans. They often gave functional reasons, but, having studied
jeans in several countries, I found that the people who claim they
are good for when it is hot are contradicted by the majority who
claim they are better for when it is cold, and those who see them
as protective against rain are challenged by those who say that
jeans are terrible in the rain, since they don't dry very quickly. The
fact that they fade might as easily have been used as evidence that
they don't last long as to make the case that they are enduring.

The single most common observation used to explain the preference for jeans is comfort, and it soon became clear that the very
word 'comfort' provides an excellent example of what social scientists call naturalisation. What this means is that people start by
using the word comfort to refer to the physical relationship to
softened cotton. There seems no reason to dispute the report that
jeans as a cotton garment feel softer and pleasanter to wear over
time. Because this is a physical transformation, we regard it as
natural. But very quickly the use of this term comfort drifts over
into social situations where people say that wearing jeans makes
them feel comfortable at a party or with certain friends. This time
the property of being comfortable has nothing to do with natural
comfort, but, because the same word is used, the effect is to make
this cultural concept of being socially comfortable seem like the
same kind of thing as the argument of comfort that stems from
the properties of cotton – which in turn means we forget that this
is a cultural observation, and the idea that denim is also socially
appropriate comes to seem like a natural property of denim itself.
In a similar manner, participants in this study defend their preference for jeans on the grounds that you don't have to wash and
iron them as often as other clothes. What they mean is that it is

socially acceptable not to wash them as often or to iron them. But there is nothing intrinsic to jeans as a textile that dictates this. We could have felt the same about corduroy or any cotton trousers, but we don't. It is just a cultural quirk that we feel we can wear dirty jeans but not dirty cords.

As I have already noted, while many women possessed branded or expensive or specially fitted jeans, often worn for special occasions, most day-to-day wearing is dominated by the most mundane and also often the cheapest of jeans. This starts to give us a picture of what it means to look ordinary. The word 'ordinary' means nondescript, nothing special; the jeans don't signify anything in particular. This is curious, since the anthropology of clothing really developed out of semiotics – that is, the study of how differences in clothing are used to mark social or cultural differences, such as male against female, rich against poor, formal against informal, and so forth.[19]

Once upon a time jeans were thoroughly semiotic. We collected some wonderful stories from some of our older informants. One Londoner thinks he was among the first men in the area to obtain a pair of blue jeans, from a US soldier during the Second World War. Another told us how his aunt was beaten up by other women in the late 1950s because she had the effrontery, as a woman, to wear a pair of jeans. For a while jeans signified the influence of America. Later on they seemed to hint at something transgressive, such as rebellious youth. But a policeman who lives in these streets told us how no one would see jeans as significant today; they prefer to look for 'hoodies' in order to predict trouble. Given the continued importance of class in Britain, it is extraordinary how jeans have lost any correspondence to income or status. Indeed, today the maid is just as likely as the mistress to wear an expensive Victoria Beckham brand of jeans.

Once, jeans were seen as appropriate to particular age groups, but not any more. A woman notes of her husband, who constantly equates being in fashion with wearing jeans:

My husband was crazy. As soon as my son was born he went and bought him some jeans that were this size. They were so uncomfortable for a baby, but he wanted to see his son in jeans right away. So he had this big nappy and this little bottom and he looked really strange. And my sister kept saying, 'You're silly, don't

be silly.' The only thing babies should be in is a babygrow or
something. We even bought him designer ones. I think it was a
really expensive pair. Ralph Polo Lauren or something. And this is
when he wasn't even walking. There was no point. You couldn't
even see the jeans. He was at six months I think. But they did grow
out very quickly and he never got to wear them.

At the other end of the spectrum, a woman talks of her 61-year-
old partner who always wears jeans because he is trim in contrast
to others of his age. He clearly sees jeans as the perfect garment
for showing off. So, even at sixty-one, he doesn't so much wear
jeans as use them to flaunt his body. 'Twice he said, if you ever
wanted to make an advert about older people in jeans, he'd be the
person to make the advert with. And that he never wears anything
else.' But most people of his age wear jeans today such that age
is no longer an issue.

If we put all this evidence together, there seems to be a good
case for viewing jeans as the first ever post-semiotic[20] garment –
the clothing that signifies nothing specific about the person who
is wearing them. Wearing jeans doesn't tell you their age, gender,
class or anything else. One of the ways we established this was
through exploring two key questions. Apart from saying that jeans
were comfortable, the other main reason people kept giving us for
why they wear blue jeans is that they 'go' with everything. There
is pretty much no garment, shoe or accessory that you can't wear
alongside jeans. This makes it a lot easier to get dressed in the
morning. So, the first question we would ask was, 'If you had
some other trousers that were exactly the same colour as blue
jeans but just not made from denim, could these trousers also go
with anything at all?' People would think about this for a while
and then come to the conclusion that they couldn't. So then we
would ask, 'If you had another pair of trousers made from denim,
but not blue, say green denim, could those go with absolutely any
other clothes?' Again people would think about this for a while
and conclude they could not.

What this demonstrates is that there is nothing intrinsic about
blue, or about denim, that makes us think that all other clothes
can go with denim blue jeans. This is a purely cultural construction and derives entirely from the fact that the dominant form of
denim blue jeans is now post-semiotic and thereby effectively

neutral. They are deprived of the ability to clash with anything they are matched with. Another piece of evidence came from the question about when or where you should not wear denim blue jeans. The answer was that, if you needed to show marked respect – for example, at a wedding or in a job where you stood in the front, serving the public – then you shouldn't wear jeans. By being unmarked, they couldn't show marked concern. But this once again shows that what blue denim jeans now signify is the state of not signifying anything, which makes them inappropriate as a means to show respect. By post-semiotic jeans I refer to the mainstream everyday jeans worn in London. These generalisations obviously do not hold for particularly expensive jeans or categories such as skinny jeans.

Now why should this matter? Well, there are many reasons, but I will select one. The area of this fieldwork was a district where, as is typical of London, there lived many people from migrant backgrounds. London has an exceptionally high percentage of migrants and is even more exceptional in the diversity and degree of dispersion of these migrants within the metropolis.[21] On these particular streets lived people from several different parts of South Asia, but also from West Africa to Latvia, from Croatia to China and the Caribbean, as well as from different parts of the United Kingdom, each area of origin essentially represented by one or two households. Taken as a whole, migrants, or their children, represented two-thirds of the participating population, making migrants typical rather than atypical of our participants.

There is a huge literature on migration and identity, and that, in a sense, is our problem. Identity implies identification, which situates migrants in arenas of choice: either to conform to and blend into the culture represented by the host society or to retain the cultural values of their place of origin. Alternatively, they can take their stance from the radical politics of Ken Livingstone, until a few years ago the leader of the Greater London Council and then mayor of London. He positively promoted multiculturalism and anti-racism, including an appreciation of various forms of syncretism and fusion. For many years, London was regarded as a centre for progressive politics regarding migration, identified specifically with the left-wing aspirations of Livingstone.

Having now carried out five ethnographies in London, I have become increasingly aware that, for many migrants, the

presumption by others of this valorisation of identity can be experienced as a burden and an imposition. Migrants are supposed to
retain roots or to represent an identity. But many of them say that
one of the major advantages of living in London, with its unusual
degree of ethnic dispersal, is that it offers a superior opportunity
for escaping from identity. For example, when I recognised that a
participant in an earlier project was from Brazil, I became interested in knowing about the aspects of his life that pertain to that
Brazilian identity. I tried to start conversations about when and
whether he eats Brazilian food or if he had Brazilian friends, to
which he responded by stating, 'If I wanted to be fucking Brazilian, I would have stayed in fucking Brazil.'[22] The great advantage
of London, with its combination of diversity and dispersal, is that,
when migrants decide to loosen an affinity with a place of origin,
they don't do so because they feel under pressure to identify with
London itself or with being British, which they might feel if living
in another part of the United Kingdom. After all, in these streets,
to come from London is a minority, not a majority, position. To
the chagrin of many more conservative or right-wing politicians,
there is in the United Kingdom relatively little explicit celebration
of a specific identity as being either British or English, compared,
at least, to identification with a local football team. By the same
token, migrants may not feel anything but a remnant or token
association with the place where they spent their childhood or
where their parents were born. Some, indeed, have an intensely
strong relationship with a place of origin, one that may grow even
if they were born in the United Kingdom. But the increasing tendency for many people is simply not to identify with a specific
cultural identity.

Once jeans achieve this post-semiotic status they become an
ideal resource for immigrants who wish to transcend identity. The
way such individuals achieve this is very rarely through any political, activist or, indeed, even conscious trajectory. Take, for example,
Odette. What makes Odette's story extraordinary is that it was so
particular to our project. The reason jeans are blue is, of course,
because of their original association with indigo. Indigo-plant
dying has almost become extinct, though it is starting to be revived
today thanks to its use for very expensive craft jeans, which also
tend to be fair-trade, organic, selvage jeans. As it happens, Odette's
family came from Sierra Leone and Gambia, and her mother, who

now lives with Odette, was herself an indigo dyer. She gave us wonderful descriptions of how she used to extract the dye from the plant and of the various resist methods by which the cloth was indigo stamped. When young, she took cloth, dyed indigo by her mother, to sell in neighbouring Liberia. Odette met her husband in France; she had one child in Sierra Leone and then two more in London. She still wears her special indigo clothing, such as wraparound skirts, for family occasions. She recently walked into Marks and Spencer and saw a set of clothes in indigo that made her feel quite homesick.

Jeans were very much in fashion during her childhood, but they came as second-hand clothes from a generic West.[23] Odette originally came to England to study at secretarial college and subsequently started to wear jeans far more often. They helped her mix in with everyone else, and she learned to dress them up for going out at night. She also bought denim skirts, jackets and jeans to send back to her daughter in Sierra Leone. For one period of her life, she wore branded jeans with labels; it was at the time when her children were young teenagers, when brands mattered to them and they wanted their mother to be seen in brand-name jeans. But then they relaxed, and she relaxed, and jeans simply became foundational wear for her and her children, especially one child, who wears jeans pretty much constantly.

Odette buys her own jeans in the United States because they are cheaper there. However, the main way jeans have become something she associates with has nothing to do with her relationship to indigo, or much to do with her relationship with her children. Rather, she comes across as rather typical of our study participants with respect to my discussion of jeans as merely comfortable. The jeans for which she has a real attachment and with which she identifies are the ones she has worn for ten years that have become soft and intimate and personal. More than just physically comfortable, they genuinely contribute to her ability to feel relaxed. But one also senses that they are part of the way she feels comfortable in the wider social sense, as just another person living in a certain North London area. She retains her marked cultural identity for those occasions when she feels this is appropriate, such as a family wedding, when she might wear clothes that signify her region of origin. Her husband is a staunch Jehovah's Witness, and she does not wear jeans for church. But in her everyday life she is content to have lost any particular regional affiliation or identity, to be mother and wife, but also to have her own career and, above all, her own personality. In most respects, she regards herself as having achieved a state of the merely ordinary, though she does not reflect much on the struggle to achieve this state.

In a few cases, migrants recall wearing jeans because they felt pressure to fit in with the host community, but mostly this was during the initial phase of migration, as may have happened with Odette. Such examples clearly do not support the general argument I am making here, but they are rare. The broader ethnographic evidence suggests that few people feel pressure to lose identity in order to conform. If anything, the opposite is the case, as there has been a clear change towards a cultural valorisation of difference, as something to cherish and celebrate on marked occasions. This is evident in the remarkable changes in the representation of difference in the popular media, such as television, and in schools, which have led to the position, exemplified by the Brazilian migrant noted above, that identity, rather than being an embarrassment, has become something of an expectation, if not a burden. You are supposed to show that at least your grandparent was African or Irish, as though this says something significant about you as a person. London, by contrast, may well represent the vanguard of something else. It has become a kind of particular nowhere – that is, a place with which one does not have to identify just in order to get away from other forms of identity. A person can state that they don't like the fact that they come from Denmark, because they don't particularly like Danes, nor are they especially fond of the British. They don't want an identity, or to be really anything other than their own personality. Most migrants today do not wear jeans either to fit in or as a mark of authentic difference. They see jeans wearing as outside of such issues of identity. For them, in their ordinariness, jeans have lost their connotations of assimilation or distinction. The term that is overwhelmingly dominant in explaining the wearing of jeans is *comfortable*.

In fact, migrants now use jeans to become and be seen as ordinary in much the same way as do non-migrants. To avoid status competition at school in the absence of a uniform, parents encourage their children to wear jeans. In college, when students wish to become part of a community without being marked, they wear jeans. When coming home from work to relax, our participants wear jeans. Jeans can be dressed up without being too dressy, but also dressed down. They resolve contradictions and deflect offence or argument. They allow people to relax into a comfortable state of ordinariness, which is not to be denigrated as a failure to become special, but is an achievement in its own right. Migrants may compare this comfort with its lack in their place of origin, seeing it as something made viable by the heterogeneity of London. As a migrant from a Gulf state noted, 'You know, here you can go out wearing ASDA jeans and Tesco jeans and you wouldn't worry. Nobody would ever say anything to you. But over there it's a big thing what you wear.' They may be aware from television that jeans are ubiquitous at a global level, but they do not assume they have the same (in)significance outside the United Kingdom, or even outside London.

Let me be clear: I am not saying that all jeans wearing in London signifies the ordinary. If that were a hypothesis, it would be a thousand times wrong.[24] Vast numbers of jeans are quite obviously worn because they are particularly stylish, have expensive labels, or effectively represent some aspects of identity and status. There are designer jeans, extraordinarily skinny jeans, highly decorated jeans, and jeans so tight women break their nails trying to button them up. The point is that these are a minority of all jeans worn. The same people who routinely wear jeans that are here categorised as ordinary often possess, and on appropriate occasions wear, designer jeans or jeans that achieve a particular effect. But none of this should detract from the significance being claimed for the majority of blue jeans, which are now worn in a manner that clearly strives to objectify a state of ordinariness. I presume that, as long as they are worn by close to a majority in the majority of countries, blue jeans will always retain that flexibility, such that some will be used to express the marked, the special and, indeed, the extraordinary. For a natural science, that use would represent a contradiction. Within an ethnography, by contrast, we can and should still assert the importance of an ordinariness that can constantly be disproved, because those exceptions do not really detract from the generalisations that apply to its dominant usage.

This example of migrants' relationship to the host society demonstrates that being ordinary is not simply something we can take for granted. There are many reasons why we actually struggle to become not extraordinary, but simply ordinary. In the recently published book[25] from which this case study is extracted we go up several more levels in our interpretation of the significance of denim blue jeans. We argue that they represent a fundamental challenge to the core theory of anthropology itself, because in anthropology we assume that people generally live according to the rules and customs of their society partly as a result of various pressures to conform and to behave appropriately – referred to as normative in the earlier chapter on shopping. But the evidence within this particular study is that people are not wearing denim blue jeans in order to conform as a result of such moral pressure. We don't generally turn to our kids and say, 'My child, when you grow up I really want you to become ordinary', or 'to wear blue jeans'. The wearing of jeans represents a different kind of social homogeneity than that which is presumed in most theory in anthropology. Ordinary is not the same as conformity.

To take this to a still higher level, we can argue that denim blue jeans represent a challenge, not just to theory in anthropology, but to the main trajectory of Western philosophy, because from Kant, through Hegel and onwards, philosophers have hoped that the Enlightenment would lead us to gain a consciousness of morality that would help us achieve moral lives through intentionality, derived from consciousness as the embodiment of reason. But if blue jeans, for example, create a degree of greater equality – and I think in some small measure they do achieve this – then it is not because of some conscious or intentional effort or morality or ideology of those who wear them. Morality is the effect and not the cause. But I don't expect to persuade anyone that denim blue jeans are a profound alternative to Kantian philosophy within a couple of paragraphs, so the interested reader will hopefully refer to the more extensive accounts.[26]

What I hope this chapter can communicate, in combination with the two previous chapters, is that consumption is a very different beast from that which appears in most other books on this topic. This only becomes evident when we force the focus upon consumption in and of itself instead of projecting upon it some other argument or cause. Goods are supplied by the market, but knowing this tells us nothing at all about why people wear blue jeans. The core traditions of social analysis applied to consumption, starting from Veblen, focused upon factors such as status difference and competition. But this factor has barely impinged on any of the last three chapters. Nor is consumption merely a map of social differences, as found in semiotic theories such as those of Barthes and Baudrillard. Rather, my study stems from the perspective of material culture as described in the book *Stuff*, which refuses to reduce objects to their symbolic relationship to persons. Instead we focus upon the way material things express our relationships and our values, sometimes as individuals, sometimes in relation to a family, as in shopping, sometimes through the forging of a highly nationalistic culture, as in Trinidadian Christmas. These values may derive from cosmology or equality, which makes the encounter with consumption more like a form of philosophical engagement. As I noted at the beginning of *Stuff*, the one thing we can be clear about as far as clothing is concerned is that it is almost never superficial, because we, the people of the contemporary world, are rarely superficial – at least if you are prepared to make the time and the effort to try and understand what we are about, instead of assuming that this is blindingly obvious. The single main problem with conventional writing about consumption is that it seems to consist largely of authors who wish to claim that they are deep by trying to show how everyone else is shallow.

5

It's the Stupid Economy

A book that deals seriously with consumption and its consequences might be expected to devote a chapter also to the wider
political economy, since it is assumed that the economy is the
major cause of consumption. In this chapter, however, I will treat
the political economy more as a consequence than a cause. One
reason some earlier studies such as those influenced by Marxism
neglected consumption was that they viewed capitalism as the
driving force, with consumption as merely an effect. If people
didn't buy all these goods, then commerce would not be profitable,
so commerce has to persuade them to shop. These assumptions
are also found in Baudrillard's early cultural studies,[1] and in
various versions throughout the social sciences and in business
studies. The exception would be textbook economics, where commerce is seen as benignly facilitating desires, all of which come
from the rational appraisal of independent consumers.

The first serious challenge to this assumption that production
causes consumption came in the 1980s from historians who discovered that the industrial revolution in Britain was in many
respects a response to changes in consumption and demand and
not, as previously assumed, the cause of these changes[2] – a huge
challenge to the way the history of that period was taught. My
own early writing on consumption[3] was largely an attempt to
direct attention to consumption as an active process of appropriation, rather than regarding it as merely the passive outcome of
economic forces. A key to such debates is our understanding of

advertising. It seems intuitively obvious that advertising exists as the mechanism to create demand in consumers, which is why companies invest in it. When I spent my year in the study of shopping I was shocked at how little advertising impinged on my findings. It seemed that only children responded directly to its blandishments. But if it had so little impact upon demand, why did companies spend so much money on it? The first part of this chapter summarises a study of the advertising industry which allowed me to answer that question. It must then follow that we have to see advertising as a consequence of consumption precisely to the degree that it is not found to be a cause of consumption. I will then argue the same for the political economy more generally, encompassing the economic side, exemplified by the rise of finance, and also the political side, which will be illustrated by the example of audit.

My aim in this chapter is not limited to some reversal of the assumed relationship between production and consumption. Having tried to change our understanding of what consumption is, I also seek to challenge our conventional view of what the economy is. Specifically I want to refute assumptions that the economy is essentially rational, scientific, intelligent, moral or immoral. Instead I want to argue that we will only understand the economy when we appreciate that it is fundamentally and quite remarkably stupid. Having made these arguments, I will then summarise the points and the connections between them, using a theory called *virtualism*, which returns us to consumption as the primary legitimation of these developments. Finally I will propose an alternative theory of value, the term which underlies most attempts to legitimise economic activity. Much of the discussion is necessarily abstract and may seem like a detour. But I believe it is crucial to our understanding of these wider consequences of consumption. When the going gets heavy, there is nothing to stop you skipping to the next chapter, which is a good deal lighter in tone.

Why advertising?[4]

It came in a whisper: a secret meeting – no one must know – but if I turned up at such and such place at such and such a time, I would discover ...? Music to an anthropologist's ear. At the very least it meant that these advertising executives trusted me. I duly turned up and, in the company of a furtive group of men, watched a series of secretly made films of naked models in the bath. Well, they might have been naked, because what we actually saw were huge quantities of soap bubbles that covered up everything bar their faces and a bit of limb. But then this meeting was all about their faces. Apparently these faces looked specifically South American rather than Italian.

The secret meeting was being called by advertising executives who worked in several South American companies for a well-known global soap brand. They were fed up with having to show imported adverts with Italian models and felt that the population of South America had the right to gawp at local models instead. To make the point, they had filmed their own adverts based on local models without informing the company headquarters, and before they revealed this secret coup to headquarters they wanted to know if Trinidad would join the revolution.

This was fun, but more importantly it helped me appreciate a much bigger issue within Trinidadian advertising. Basically, Trinidadian advertising was thriving, with several strong, well-staffed agencies, some affiliated with international groups such as Saatchi and Saatchi and especially McCann Erickson, but also other entirely local firms. But after a while I began to realise that they really shouldn't have been thriving. Much of the advertising was for established global brands, such as Lever Brothers, Coca-Cola and Nestlé. From the point of view of these corporations, maximum profits would be retained if they made their advert in one place, say Germany or the US, and then sent these out as what are termed *canned* advertising to local agencies around the world, who then simply placed them in the best media slots. In which case, a local agency really needed a staff of only around two.

Obviously this would not have made those local advertising agencies particularly happy. But the only way to change the situation was to persuade these corporations that the Trinidad market was so special and idiosyncratic that such global adverts could not possibly appeal; that the only way to sell these goods was to make their adverts locally. Trinidadians, whom I have always regarded as the smartest people on the planet, were very, very good at this. As a result the majority of adverts shown on Trinidadian TV were locally produced. Now, if you are actually having to make your own adverts rather than merely showing imported canned adverts, you needed a huge staff and lots of money. For the anthropologist there was a delicious irony here. Given the way these companies had legitimated their expenditure, it followed that any adverts they produced needed to be saturated with local content and images to differentiate them from the global adverts they were replacing. So it seemed that the main promoters of Trinidadian cultural distinctiveness and difference had actually become the advertisers of global brands. The irony was that, in social science, global brands are constantly assumed to be the progenitors of global homogeneity, crushing local distinctiveness. I had found quite the opposite.

Some of this responded to what I too regarded as the local appropriation of goods such as Coca-Cola, but in other cases the global adverts may well have been more effective. It was rather the self-interest of the agencies that was pushing localisation. The net result was that global corporations were spending far more, and quite possibly earning a little less, than would otherwise be the case. This was typical of my study of commerce. Instead of some seamless, intelligent and rational entity, commerce actually consists of all sorts of interest groups riddled with intriguing internal contradictions. The point was already established in chapter 2, where we saw how the local franchise for Coca-Cola is always struggling against the authority of the global company.

Contradictions were also integral to the very structure of the advertising agencies, most especially the conflict between those called *account managers*, who answered to the clients of the agency, and those called *creatives*, who wanted a reputation for clever and artistic adverts. The former spent their time plastering the brand logos all over the adverts and the latter spent their time taking these brand logos out again. Sometimes it was a clash between textbook ideology and practice. Trinidadian agency executives tend to be trained in North American colleges with typical business textbooks. When they returned they dutifully argued for the local liberalisation of the media, even though that would be catastrophic for their own interests, since such a dispersed media would be much more dependent upon imported programmes and less able to pay for expensive locally made adverts. My monograph on the ethnography of capitalism[5] has many more examples

of such contradictions. It showed that contradictions and problems rarely arose from any lack of intelligence or ability in the
people who work in advertising, but derives from the conflicted
system within which they have to work.

Indeed, this can ring true for the industry as a whole. My key
question was: why did companies spend so much money on an
industry that seemed so rarely to deliver? Some products did well,
some did badly, but the reasons seemed more to do with the
product itself or developments in consumer style. After sitting in
countless meetings, I realised that advertising budgets were rarely
being justified in terms of the impact on consumers. Inevitably the
arguments were made on the basis of the advertising expenditure
of rival companies. While no one could demonstrate that advertising worked, no one could show that it didn't. Most standard
products have been around for ages anyway, and it was pretty
hard to make a dent in them. Most new products fail, but the
reasons for this could be anything from the packaging or accessibility to the quality of the product. It was very hard to separate
out the advertising as an independent variable. But there are
exceptions. Sometimes it was possible to show that a specific
advertising campaign had had a major and positive impact on
sales, though often this was in shifting between two rival brands
rather than changing demand for the product per se. So there was
always the fear that, if the rival company was heavily invested in
advertising, then you should be too. As a result, some product
sectors had very little advertising, while others spent vast amounts.
But you would also expect advertising to be pretty good at advertising itself, as just demonstrated by the ability of Trinidadian
advertising to persuade the world's biggest corporations to pay
for entirely unnecessary local advertising. This wasn't quite *Mad
Men*,[6] but advertising retains a certain glamour. So one could see
how, in practice, it was possible for advertising to thrive as an
industry and yet conclude that, if advertising ceased to exist, the
overall demand for goods would probably be largely unaffected.
This wasn't because demand came from rational choice, as economists believe. It was because goods, quite apart from those such
as cars and computers that enhance our capacities, are highly
expressive of relationships and culture and are extremely nuanced,
as demonstrated in my last three chapters. These chapters explain

where demand comes from without requiring any reference to advertising.

I don't want to overswing the pendulum. There is, of course, evidence that people in marketing and advertising can sometimes alter our preferences and create demand. There are many books written by industry insiders replete with statistics showing sales before and after a campaign. There are not so many books that document their failures, though most new products do fail. My own evidence from the study of shopping and of the industry suggests that advertising is actually very effective at creating demand when it comes to children. Indeed, I strongly advocate abolishing all advertising aimed at children, which very likely has damaging consequences. By contrast, my evidence is that ending advertising to adults would be largely inconsequential with respect to the demand for consumer goods.

The subsequent relationship between advertising and the consumer could sometimes be even more bizarre. In Trinidad, advertising agencies didn't want to offend people, so typically they picked models of mixed race, rather than having to choose one who was clearly Indian or African. Since part of my research consisted of watching adverts with consumers to gauge their response, I could see that the Indian population was incensed by what they saw as a conspiracy by commerce and the government to promote a mixed-race ideal in the teeth of Indian endogamy – the principle that Indians should marry only other Indians. In trying to avoid offence they caused much more.

The selectivity of viewers was also remarkable. I followed in some detail a campaign for a soya milk drink called Supligen, marketed by Nestlé, one of the clearest illustrations of Trinidadian agency's most common idiom, which was to sell on the theme of sex. The television advert consisted of a female in a leotard working out, as though in a gym, followed by a male with rippling muscles operating a pneumatic drill between his legs. The female is shown throwing a carton of Supligen to the male and giving a clear wink to the viewer as they leave together through a door made from a Supligen pack. The pack itself is based on the profile of what might be taken to be a comet, but is clearly also intended to be taken as a penis in action. The slogan to the advert is 'The nourishment behind performance', and the off-screen voice notes,

'It will help you perform longer'. The merchandising associated the drink with free packets of peanuts or chickpeas, both of which are traditionally supposed to help men sustain their sexual drive. An example is the oft-quoted cry of street-corner peanut sellers – 'Bullets for your gun!' The advertising executives with whom I worked had no reticence in confirming sex as the substance of their strategy.

In reading the last paragraph, could sex have been more explicit? Yet the viewers of these TV adverts simply refused to see Supligen as associated with sex in any way at all. All they ever saw were messages about the drink giving nourishment and help in strenuous work or leisure activities – but not sex. Typical responses were 'It's a sort of health drink, shows people working hard' or 'They just put someone there to show he is doing a good job after he drinks it. He is very energetic, he is doing something very hard. I don't see any other thing in it. The package – I think it's a light bulb.' No such reticence was shown with other advertisements that sold on sex.

The explanation became apparent when the executives looked at the sales. While these were reasonably good, it was found that the primary use of Supligen was in school lunch-boxes for children, where it was regarded as more sustaining than the usual milk drinks, especially for their brains. Clearly the last thing the consumers wanted to 'see' in respect to their schoolchildren was sex. This begs some fascinating anthropological questions about how groups determine meaning and usage as a collective, often outside of pressures from commerce. But the more immediate point, once again, is to question the idea that there is some kind of seamless relationship between active commerce and passive consumers.

By now my understanding of advertising had drifted far from the textbooks. I was seeing advertising more as a side consequence than a cause of consumption. As a result, I was starting to wonder how far these findings of contradictions and conflicting interest groups and ideologies would also work for the larger economy. As it happens, at that time Trinidadian companies were also doing rather well. I was astonished to find that the two largest transnational corporations in the area were home-grown Trinidadian corporations. Neal and Massy and ANSA McAL were among the biggest companies in the Caribbean. The former had nearly 7,000 employees, while companies such as Lever Brothers or Nestlé had around 500 each. Their main current problems were not commercial. Rather they were suffering from the influence of a higher realm of economic thought. The fashion current at that time within global economics was for *structural adjustment*. Developed partly in response to the opening up of the ex-Soviet bloc, it subjected countries to the full rigours of an economic theory which saw all local concerns as distortions of the free market, whether protectionism, currency control or even decent welfare provision. In my book on capitalism I show how these two come into constant conflict. The forces that directly reflected top-down economic theory, a sort of pure capitalism, were inimical to the actual successful practices of these major companies.[7]

This was partly because Trinidadian capitalism worked in quite a locally specific fashion. I had been educated about something called *capitalism* where the very word implied a homogeneous logic. The problem had been that both the proponents and the critics of capitalism join in the conspiracy to simplify the propositions represented by the word 'capitalism'. This ethnographic study revealed that I should have been talking about capitalisms in the plural. With this changed perspective the world looked different. In reading more widely, I found that pension fund capitalism works for the UK, but in Germany the banks occupy that critical position of ownership, while in China it is the state and most especially regional state governments. With respect to the last, the fact that today's most successful capitalism appears to be communist capitalism is surely worth a pause for further academic thought about what this word means. There remain all sorts of local particularities and regulatory systems.[8] Just as I had found with advertising, these sometimes work reasonably well, and the people within them are intelligent and opportunistic enough to develop a myriad pattern of little interest groups and competitive advantages. Sometimes they come into contradiction and create crises. But the idea that there is some overarching intelligence, rationality or morality is not supported by this evidence – if there is a wizard, it's the wizard of Oz.

All of this emerged from the fact that I was studying commerce ethnographically. There is some confirmation in that contradiction also appears as the primary conclusion of other ethnographic studies, even when they go upwards to the higher realms of global finance. The central point of Ho's ethnography of Wall Street[9] is that the ideal of shareholder value rendered capitalism itself schizophrenic, riven by two competing visions: one that of the corporation as a social entity, as seen from the perspective of corporate management, and the other of the corporation as a financial property, as seen from the perspective of stock markets. In a very similar fashion it is contradiction that becomes the main focus of Ouroussoff,[10] who devotes her ethnography to the rating agencies that occupy another pivotal position in the economy. In her case, the key contradiction was that company executives are completely aware that it is impossible actually to quantify the risk of loss that resulted from investments, but, since no one would actually invest in companies without this so-called evidence, they simply acquiesced in the supply of apparent figures, which, like so much in the financial system, merely adds to the obfuscation that is a contributory cause of periodic crises. So, if these different contributions of detailed ethnographic work by anthropologists studying what the economy actually does, rather than what it is supposed to do, seem to conclude that contradiction is the norm at every level, why is the economy represented as quite the opposite?

Beliefs, epistemology and economics

When I started trying to understand business, economics and finance, I turned to what seemed an authoritative guide. It was a book called *Mastering Finance*.[11] It carried the imprimatur of the *Financial Times* and several of the world's leading business schools. Its declared principal topic is *value*, claiming that, 'In theory, stocks are claims on real assets: capital and land, which derive their value from the sale of real goods and services.'[12] The words 'in theory' may explain why this is about the only time such assets are mentioned. The book is really dominated by the concept of *risk* as applied to investment decisions. It establishes a moral agenda in which 'investors are receiving a premium for exposure to equity market risk'.[13] It is a moral imperative that markets should reward investors for accepting risk.

This is a morality said to be based on science, because the market is an efficient system, a technology that can transform knowledge into value. Miyazaki[14] shows how Japanese arbitrage traders make money by noticing when prices show a discrepancy from their *correct* market level. But they are also moral agents who punish such deviations, re-establishing the market as efficiency. As a science, economists can measure and model various kinds of risk, which may derive from the volatility of a company or the volatility of the market as a whole. This measure is called *beta*. Ideally, past performance can help predict future performance; portfolios will then become more effective and risk largely eliminated.

Unfortunately the real world misbehaves: 'The reality seems to indicate investors who purchased high beta stocks have not achieved a higher rate of return than investors who purchased low beta stocks.'[15] Similarly, historical records show that, in the long run, stocks have generally been less risky than bonds.[16] Small stocks give excessive returns against large stocks,[17] while dividends are not supposed to affect price, but clearly do so.[18] So this textbook is in effect comprised of three elements. The dominant form is the presentation of finance as an overarching system that should be taught as a science replete with equations. The second element in the background is that somehow this science is also a morality designed to reward people who behave in particular ways, such as taking risks. Thirdly, there is the largely suppressed but nevertheless present evidence that, so far, actual markets quite often simply don't behave in the way that this science and this morality assumes. This third element is not allowed to impinge much on the other two. Even more strikingly, there is no allowance for what could be called common sense. For example, no one outside of academic economics would be surprised that markets reflect dealers' feelings of confidence. Nor would the rest of us believe that there is no particular economic advantage in actually controlling a company.[19] But, according to such textbooks, there cannot be any such advantage, since that would contradict the ideal of efficient markets.[20]

To understand what is going on here we need a brief excursion to a debate about epistemology, or the theory of what knowledge is. Such debate is rare today but dominated when I started my career as a student of archaeology.[21] Epistemology has an extraordinary power to divide and to control the world we live in. Put simply, the last three centuries have seen the triumph of natural science, evident in a thousand things we now take for granted. Natural science studies the non-cultural world, where rules can be universal and predictable and experiments repeated. We recognise the cultural nature of science as practice, as argued by Latour[22] and others, but, when a new medicine is being created or an aircraft part tested, we are generally comfortable with the idea that this rests upon theories of how knowledge develops through models, analysis, repetition, experiment and proof. I will not bite the hand of science, which, for example, through the green revolution, fed billions of people who would otherwise have experienced starvation.[23] The practice of science is clearly culturally inflected and infused, but that is not a refutation of its desire to retain transcendent criteria for differentiating good from bad science.

Given this vast success, it is no surprise that many academics in other fields wish to be associated with that degree of reputation and sense of certainty. But the theories of natural science work to the extent that its objects of study are physical forces which are subject to predictable and replicable situations. I believe it is entirely inappropriate to assume that would ever be the case in cultural practices such as discussing how best to bring up children or deciding which car to buy. But economics (often with the support of psychology, which works along the same epistemological lines) aspires to experimentation, modelling, replicable processes and proof. It is this aspiration that explains why a textbook on finance is written the way it is. It is epistemology that explains why so much economic (and, indeed, psychological) work tends to lack much bearing on the world we actually live in.

Those steeped in the epistemology of natural science find little value in the kind of work I do. They see no samples, no hypothesis, no proofs – nothing that they can regard as evidence or scholarship. They really can't see why anyone would ever fund such research, which, given their dominant positions in academia, explains why such funding has almost entirely disappeared in the UK. By contrast, I see huge numbers of very well-funded artificial experiments on human behaviour, economic, psychological and otherwise, which to my mind tell us very little about the behaviour of real people in the actual world we live in, because one cannot extrapolate from models and experiments how people behave in their everyday lives. I resent that vast amounts of money are wasted on such work. Things may merge at the boundaries, but 'hard' economists and 'soft' anthropologists would rarely bother reading each other's work or journals these days. I wish things were not so black and white, but I have not seen any dilution of this fundamental impasse during my career as a professional academic. These academics assume that, if I don't apply their kind of science, then I must be some kind of pure relativist who will equally accept anything. I fully believe in social science and the necessity of patient and extensive observation. In turn, this also ensures anthropology is rarely used by commerce, because the timetables of commerce are rarely built to allow for spending at least a year in scholarly study before making statements about one's findings. There is no such thing in anthropology as a short ethnography.[24] I see a clear contrast between knowledge and ignorance, between education and supposition, and my job consists of educating students in the many ways scholarship can contribute to understanding.

Economics might have been a social science based on similar scholarly observation of how commerce actually works. But it chose instead to emulate the natural sciences, orientated to modelling aggregate and largely decontextualised data that would allow the discourse of experiment and proof and mathematics. The kinds of ethnographic studies I have just cited, which are becoming common across anthropology, sociology and human geography, are dismissed because we are not scientists. So textbooks such as *Mastering Finance* are exercises in imagining the science that might have existed had the market been a rational and efficient laboratory process. If one reads the language of economics, or what McCloskey calls the rhetoric of economics,[25] it becomes evident how they have also added this further component, a rather simplistic morality with its own system of punishment and reward. The situation is not that different in some Marxist economics, which also start from a claim to the science of value, but in that case based on an unswerving insistence upon the inherent immorality, rather than an inherent morality, of markets.

This is not a book about economics, and I fully acknowledge the level of overgeneralisation that such a brief excursion involves. I am focusing here on the dominant forms of economic theory that give rise to the textbooks most students have to read and be examined on in order to qualify in economics. But economics is a vast field, and there are in addition many other kinds of economics, from feminist, through post-autistic, Keynesian, behavioural, green and others, as well as many far less crude left-wing critics than those I have glibly categorised as Marxist. Within these alternatives, there is a growing concern to provide something closer to what I have advocated through the example of ethnographic studies of commercial practice, with names such as 'real-world economics'.[26] A serious student would spend time educating themselves in these alternatives.

'Stuff happens' in aggregate[27]

Apart from ethnography by social scientists, there are two major sources for an alternative viewpoint which would help us shift from these distortions of pseudo-science to a more genuinely informed view of how the economy actually works. One source is critical writing by alternative economists, and in this capacity Marxist-orientated authors, such as David Harvey, are particularly useful. In the aftermath of the 2008 banking crisis it became clear that there has to be some sort of connection between the world of consumption and advertising and the monstrous system of banking and finance – but how do they connect? According to the textbooks, the key to the relationship is the stock market, which exists to provide capital to firms. Fortunately there are good critical studies which tell another story. In his book on Wall Street,[28] Doug Henwood shows that quite the opposite was a good deal more true. In the period before the recent crash, firms could get much higher returns investing in finance than investing in actual commerce. So they did. 'Between 1952 and 1997 almost all (92%) of business investment was paid for by the firms' own cash',[29] while 'between 1981 and 1997, US nonfinancial corporations retired $813 billion more in stock than they issued, thanks to takeovers and buybacks'.[30] The smaller firms that would really benefit from an ability to raise capital from the markets found those markets quite unsympathetic and largely conducted their borrowing under the harsher regimes imposed by their primary source of finance, which was the banking system.[31] So, instead of money going downwards to fund business, profits were being channelled upwards to feed this self-perpetuating money machine in high finance. In conclusion, Henwood is able to argue that 'the U.S. financial system performs dismally at its advertised task, that of efficiently directing society's savings toward their optimum investment pursuits. The system is stupefyingly expensive, gives terrible signals for the allocation of capital, and has surprisingly little to do with real investment.'[32] It turns out this is quite an old story. At several points Henwood quotes Keynes, who also argued that financial markets are 'irrational, destabilizing, and paradoxically conservative institutions that do more to expand rentier wealth than they do to nourish a broad and secure prosperity',[33] or that 'Speculators may do no harm as bubbles on a steady stream of enterprise. But the position is serious when enterprise becomes the bubble on a whirlpool of speculation. When the capital development of a country becomes the by-product of the activities of a casino, the job is likely to be ill-done.'[34] So, just as consumption legitimates much commercial practice such as retail and advertising, these firms in turn legitimate the development of higher financial sectors, which then engage mainly in quite other activities. Once again, it is helpful if we see finance more as a consequence than as a cause.

What the critics don't usually provide is that sense of direct observation at the human level that ethnographers tend to demand. But in addition there is also excellent qualitative observational work on actual financial practice by insiders that seem to support these perspectives. Some of the best economic journalism gives us the level of detail we expect from fine-grained ethnography. Examples regarded as classics of this genre include *Barbarians at the Gate*[35] or Michael Lewis's *Liar's Poker*.[36] These accounts are full of larger than life characters who exhibit behaviour a million miles from the models of the textbooks. What they possess is cunning, bluff and the ability to second guess the intentions of the other.

The same Michael Lewis who wrote *Liar's Poker* more recently published a book called *The Big Short*.[37] In finance, people make money largely by predicting correctly what the market will do. It follows that, if the crash of 2008 had been some sort of conspiracy, or at least predictable, then these shrewd people working in investment could have made an absolute fortune betting on this outcome. In fact hardly anyone did. Lewis's book is about the mere ten to twenty persons[38] whom his research suggests actually understood the implications of subprime mortgages and did make money betting against them. He contrasts them with the many thousands who didn't see this coming even when the evidence was all around them. Even experienced and clever financiers could fail to understand entirely something called 'a synthetic subprime mortgage bond-backed collateralized debt obligation'.[39] But this didn't stop them from trading in such instruments, a blindness facilitated by the vast incentives they derived from not allowing themselves an intelligent inspection. If I use the word 'stupid', Lewis's book is replete with terms such as 'moronic' and 'imbecilic'. But his invective reflects an entirely reasonable anger with a *mistake* that maybe cost around a trillion dollars – though a trillion that probably shouldn't have existed in the first place.[40] But, more to the point, this also led to countless individual stories of suffering, starting from those who were cruelly misled into thinking they had fulfilled an aspiration to home ownership, only subsequently literally to lose the plot. You might also note that there are no equations or models in Lewis's book, just the insights that come from high-grade qualitative information.

For economics textbooks, the markets are intrinsically rational, but those who play them are not, and so such books can admit that investors will indulge in things like irrational exuberance. Yet what Henwood and Lewis reveal are some very clever operators. What caused irrational exuberance and collapse was not the stupidity of the traders but the internal contradictions and absurdities of markets. When I use the term 'stupidity' to describe this system, it implies that markets themselves usually work blind without much real understanding or intelligence. This is mainly a result of their own complexity and the fortuitous contradictions of the forces that have been created. Even the US Treasury finds that its actions have unexpected impacts upon institutions, because it has limited control over them or finds it difficult to predict what they will do. This applies not just to stock market fluctuations but to the impact of forces such as currency exchanges, commodity prices, the rise of China and many, many others.

Still, the word 'stupid' represents a pretty strong claim as a characterisation of the economy as a whole. I therefore want to follow this with two other examples that help bolster the case. My second example rests on a rather simple and obvious question about contemporary capitalism: who owns it? In my original studies in Marxism I had been schooled in the fundamental opposition between capitalism and the proletariat. Yet by the end of the twentieth century the correct answer to who owns British capitalism turned out to be – the proletariat. About 45 per cent of all the quoted equities in the UK are owned by pension funds and life insurance companies. Given the fragmentation of most of the remaining ownership, in effect these companies could be said to own most of British capitalism. These are the pensions and insurance funds held primarily in trust for workers.

The reasons are once again largely fortuitous. Pensions and insurance companies have to be backed by vast sums in order to meet their future obligations, and will be expected to invest these funds as profitably as they can. As we have seen, it's the markets which were giving the best returns, so they invest in capitalism. Fortunately we have an excellent study of this: *Pension Fund Capitalism*,[41] by the geographer Gordon Clark. At first, ownership was merely passive, but increasingly pension-fund managers were called upon to become more actively involved, otherwise they could find themselves blamed for poor investment strategies by the likes of the British chancellor of the exchequer. So, 'Increasingly, they demand a voice in the companies in which they invest – for instance, a veto over board appointments, executive compensation, and critical corporate charter provisions.'[42] This leads to a situation in which it is the managers of pension funds rather than the actual CEOs of companies who are in a position ultimately to determine the way those companies are run.

But what Clark then reveals is a situation that would be breathtakingly funny if the consequences were not rather serious. Pension funds are managed by trustees, often appointed representatives of the plan's beneficiaries. But, historically, many firms had seen being a pension-fund trustee as a pretty harmless position to which one could shunt individuals in management who were not doing a particularly good job, but whom you didn't want to fire. A really good manager was best retained in active management within the company itself. So it was more than likely that these trustees were from the least competent component of firms. Furthermore, 'All the evidence from the Anglo-American world is that most trustees begin their term relatively ignorant of investment theory and practice.'[43] This didn't matter so much when they were just passive

shareholders. But gradually people who may not have been particularly competent and had little knowledge of investment were
becoming the ultimate owners and thereby decision-makers of the
most powerful companies in the UK. Once again, this example of
stupidity was not intentional but simply the fortuitous outcome
of complex relationships.

If company CEOs were ceding authority to pension-fund managers on one side, much of the rest of their authority was slipping
away towards another curious late entry into capitalism, the management consultants. Just as was the case with pension funds, this
took even the consultants by surprise. I interviewed an individual
who had over twenty years of service in one of the key consultancy
firms. Her own training was in accountancy, which was her firm's
primary concern when she joined it. But, increasingly, she found
herself drawing up wider plans for her clients and mutating into
a consultant, even though she had no training for that work. At
first she could just make her case and then exit. But then firms felt
that, having spent so much money on consultants' reports, the
consultants ought to take more responsibility for implementation,
putting such new systems into place. This is what she was now
doing.

She reflects the larger story of firms such as Andersen Consulting, originally a spin-off from an accountancy firm, Arthur
Andersen, but which by 1995 had an annual income of US$4.2
billion and employed 44,000 people, with 152 offices in 47
countries. In historical terms this happened 'overnight'. Between
1980 and 1987 the revenue of registered management consultancy grew fivefold, concurrent with the rise of management
gurus, business schools, management seminars and other examples of what Thrift has called *soft capitalism*.[44] Management consultancy had become a major recruiter of university graduates
and was increasingly used by CEOs to shift the blame for difficult
decisions and problematic results, perhaps the primary reason
they were prepared to spend so much on them. Companies
such as McKinsey then started to advise not just firms but governments and international bodies. Indeed, there are some grounds
for considering McKinsey to be the world's most powerful
company today. I know several families whose bright young children with top university degrees were recruited to management
consultancy jobs despite having no experience of business. So, as

in the profession of economics, it is usually the most intelligent and impressive individuals who are turned into these instruments of relative incompetence. O'Shea and Madigan,[45] who described this transformation, have used instructive sources, such as the accounts of court cases where management consultants have been sued, to shed considerable doubt as to what, if anything, companies gain from this vast expenditure on what they call 'dangerous company'.

It may seem that we have strayed far from the world of consumption, but, when we look more closely at such companies, we will find the main driver behind their work to be remarkably familiar from consumption studies. Above all, consultancy is a fashion industry. Consultants have to persuade companies that they have the latest ideas about what will make them successful. A typical example of such a fashion was called *shareholder value*. According to this, a sensible company should stop paying attention to minor issues, such as profitability, and instead concentrate all their efforts on maintaining and growing their stock market value. If someone knew nothing about business and was trained only in the kind of textbook I described above, this makes complete sense. They have read that the market is a rational system which efficiently translates everything that is known about a firm into value, so that must be the proper measure of the company's performance. The fashion was grounded in a series of quasi-academic business texts[46] which gave the appropriate *metrics* by which value could be measured and instructions about how to implement the necessary changes. For example, in 1995 some senior figures in McKinsey wrote *Valuation: Measuring and Managing the Value of Companies.*[47] Valuation is proposed as merely a natural advance in the evolution of methods for making businesses run more effectively. 'Beneath the techniques and methods we present lies the belief that maximising shareholder value is or ought to be the fundamental goal of all businesses.'[48] 'Focusing on shareholder value is not a one-time task to be done only when outside pressure from shareholders emerges or potential acquirers emerge. It is an ongoing initiative.'[49] Traditional measures such as profitability are held to be mere smokescreens that disguise the real goal of shareholder value.

If management consultants were the missionaries of shareholder value as fashion, then an ethnography by the anthropologist Karen

Ho[50] reveals their powers of conversion. She confronted share-holder value, established at the heart of the investment banks, which in turn lie at the heart of finance. The concept had become ubiquitous, such that the people she worked with could not allow themselves to conceive of the idea that there might be a contradiction between the interests of corporations and an unswerving devotion to increasing the value of their stocks.[51] Much of her ethnography is concerned with the question 'How did my informants explain the real-world failures of the strategies that were supposed to achieve shareholder value?'[52]

There were many negative results. One of the consequences has been the dominance of short-term thinking; since company acquisition could be so rapid, one could no longer afford temporary weakness.[53] There was an appeal to quick measures that could boost stock prices. This often took the form of cost-cutting, principally through downsizing – that is, the reduction of the workforce, often leading to the collapse of key components such as decent customer services and a general demoralisation. An ever increasing percentage of profits went to shareholders as dividends and growing pay packets for managers, with subsequently less money going into actual investment. Another tactic was companies using their profits to buy back their own equities, which, as a result of being both in demand and less available, tended to rise in value. This strategy became known as the leveraged buy-out and forms the narrative of *Barbarians at the Gate*.

It is not just contradictions that plague economic structures but also this increasing orientation to fashion. Reading Ho, one can also sense the power of McCloskey's[54] arguments about the *rhetoric* in economic language. Considering my own evidence with regard to how advertising actually operates in Trinidad, together with the evidence from pension-fund capitalism and the rise of management consultancy, the term 'stupidity' seems a reasonable generalisation for at least some of the practices across the entire gamut of the economy, from the workings of firms to that of the political economy as a whole. Apparently Jack Welch, the then chairman of General Electric, who was credited with inventing the term 'shareholder value', has more recently declared it probably the dumbest idea in the world.[55]

Davies[56] gives a very helpful summary of thirty-eight candidates one could blame for the recent banking crisis. Among his rogue's gallery there are several that rest upon the ideologies that pervade the discipline of economics and the teaching of business schools, including their belief in efficient markets and the dominance of the more purist Chicago School.[57] It's a little comforting to learn that there is now a 'Paul Wooley Centre for the Study of Capital Market Dysfunctionality'[58] at the London School of Economics. That should be one busy little centre. I personally would put a bit more emphasis upon companies, such as McKinsey, and the true Dolce and Gabbana nature of management consultants, who flog the latest styles in business management, telling firms that they would look quite dreadful if they were even to think of going public unless they come out dressed in finest shareholder value. Yet the aggregate effect of these fashions was not at all pretty.

These three examples are intended to show not that the entirety of the economy is stupid – that would itself be a stupid claim – but that we are much better placed to understand the economy if we start from this presumption of stupidity rather than the current assumption of intrinsic intelligence, rationality or, indeed, morality. As should be clear by now, I am politically a sort of Norwegian social democrat. I am not advocating an alternative to capitalism. People and firms obviously require banks and capital and complex global trade. Current levels of consumption would not be possible without them. And, yes, we certainly do need economists who have the training in quantitative techniques that may be appropriate to deciding when interest rates should come down or the likely impact on inflation of a new tax, and have a deep knowledge of many factors that I, for one, do not pretend to possess. Fortunately there is a trend away from this more puritan version of economic theodicy,[59] perhaps best exemplified by the respect given to Amartya Sen, a Nobel prize winning economist who clearly subjects these means to a focus upon the ends of wider human welfare and takes a dismissive stance to much of the given doctrine, including rational choice theory.[60] There has always been an alternative strand within economics, from John Maynard Keynes to Joseph Stiglitz to Real World Economics. I have been trying to show you some pretty disgusting bathwater, but I don't advocate throwing out the baby. I take my underlying position from Hegel's *Philosophy of Right*.[61] All human institutions that serve us also have an intrinsic tendency to an autonomy, through which they come to serve their own interests at our expense. This is why I want briefly to show that precisely the same arguments apply if we turn from the economic side of political economy to the political.

Best value?[62]

If commerce has been transformed over several decades by the rise of management consultants and pension funds, then, working as an academic in the public service, I bore witness to an equally powerful and apparently unstoppable force. This was the rise of audit. Once upon a time I happily spent many hours discussing academic work with students. But, increasingly, this direct involvement in education was replaced by an orientation to huge new audit systems with names such as Quality Teaching Assurance or the REF.[63] The university managements were telling us that everything we did had to be geared to success measured in the terms of these audits. Rather like performance targets elsewhere, if something wasn't audited there was no reason to do it. The connection with the previous discussion is partly that such audits represented an attempt by the state to claim it was imposing the same disciplines and forms of scientific efficiency as commerce. After a while, it was clear that there was nothing much an individual academic could do to prevent this assault on their academic work, at least without clear evidence that the consequences were very different from those intended – which would require an ethnography.[64]

If I was going to audit an audit ethnographically, I might as well go for the biggest. In 2001 this turned out to be something intriguingly called Best Value, an audit of every local government service in England.[65] I turned up at their headquarters and asked if I could join their teams of inspectors as an observer, which was agreed. I subsequently learnt a great deal about libraries, rubbish collection, IT services and the maintenance of parks. The point of the audit was that, even if the government felt councils were good value, it needed to prove this to its critics. These days the arbitrators tend to be economists, so audit has lost its qualitative side and deteriorated into a question of measurement associated with various new forms of quantification and performance targets. But these measures were being applied to highly qualitative experience, feelings about rubbish collections or the flowers in parks.

The intention was to force local government to pay attention to the demands of the electorate. A few days of inspecting showed how much this was already true. Local government still retains something of the Weberian sense of service to the community.[66] Workers in this sector may accept poorer salaries and conditions of service than those in the private sector because they can take pride in service to the community. However, in practice, an audit takes them from their orientation to local populations, replacing this with a concern to satisfy audit inspectors. The way the workers put it, they no longer feel they 'own the process'.

So, for all its good intentions, Best Value ends up having the reverse of its intended effect. An ethnography can show how this happens. Best Value was couched in terms of the four C's: Councils must Challenge how and why their service is provided, Compare with others, embrace fair Competition and Consult with users. To save space I will take just two of these. Challenge is directed at the fundamental *raison d'être* for any particular section. It sought to create a clear, jargon-free set of aims and to reduce bureaucracy and process in favour of delivering goals. Technically, you had to show how service performance will reach the top quartile for all councils over the next five years. But, given the overwhelming importance of Best Value, what this produced in practice was a new cadre of specialist Best Value officers hired to teach each local government service in turn how to get through the process with high marks. These experts actually generated an additional level of jargon. Unlike academic jargon, which tends to obfuscation, this jargon is a parody of transparency – endless pages of formulae with neither substantive content nor examples, such as 'For local government, effective performance management requires co-ordinated planning and review systems that enable key decision makers, both political and managerial, to take action based on facts about performance.'[67] So Best Value Challenge, which aimed to cut bureaucracy and jargon, actually ended up creating an additional level.

Similarly, Best Value was devoted to getting councils to Consult with the public. The Best Value report was supposed to provide the evidence for consultation and its subsequent use in determining aims, priorities and delivery. So I would watch them round up a bunch of hapless citizens and subject them to what was called a pin-point focus group aimed at extracting their priorities. Now, much of what local government does is of limited interest to the public, and citizens are not trained in interpreting long-term planning for transport, but they may have slipped on dog-poo. So they disregarded the mayor's transport plan and put dog-poo as their priority. Furthermore, councils are told everything must be justified as consumer demands, but they also have to implement government policy. In practice the poor old local council is now responsible for properly 'educating' the public, so that the latter will apparently of their own volition 'choose' recycling as their priority, which then fits and legitimates the new government policy. What happens is that actual consulting increasingly gets replaced by the need to represent action as being based on consulting. This was quite familiar from my own work, where I watch students mindlessly fill out log books that represent a process of supervision as something audited but which takes time from anyone actually supervising anyone else.

Similar contradictions worked their way through every facet of Best Value. Overall it was intended to save money, but councils calculated it added about 2.5 per cent to their costs. If the targets had at least stayed in place for many years it would have given some consistent measures, but it was inevitable that Best Value itself would soon be replaced by a different audit with different targets and languages. I thought the funniest (or saddest) moment was when inspectors said that there was now a new level playing field between private suppliers and local government, so that consumers would get the most effective service. But the inspectors then managed to argue that the private suppliers were more cost-effective because they didn't have all the additional costs and demands of bureaucratic red tape, such as...Best Value inspections. I only wish I was making that up.

Politics is full of highly intelligent, rational and, in this case I would argue (against the common grain), unusually moral participants. Working closely with both, I became convinced by the conscientiousness and moral integrity of both council workers and inspectors, who otherwise get a terrible press. The problem is, again, not the people, but how processes, with the best intentions, can develop abstract and autonomous characteristics that make them into the exact opposite of what they are supposed to be and end up with results best described as stupid. So this term applies to the political economy, not just the economy.

How the virtual came to create the real[68]

Turning from economics to politics helps lead us back to the place of consumption in causing these consequences. Audit rose to prominence based on a discourse to which consumption was central. It implied a new concern for consumer rights and consumer authority. Fields such as medicine and education were genuinely lacking in answerability to those who used their services, and my view would be that, initially, audit improved the quality of services and increased concern for patients and students. But the push to audit came from the right of the political spectrum, with a strong preference towards commercial provision as against that of the state, and pushed audit to an extreme, undermining professional authority.[69] The ideal of consulting consumers became reduced to focus groups, assuming with any evidence that ordinary consumers would be fully able to appraise complex government policy. As in contemporary California, where citizens happily vote simultaneously for lower taxes and higher services, you can have too much democracy, including consumer democracy.

As a result, within the university context, audit had stopped being about how to be concerned with students and became a series of mechanisms that could represent the ideal of being concerned, in some quantified fashion. Today academics have to spend time trying to force reluctant students to fill out feedback forms on our performance, because they no longer see any point in such forms. This replacement of actual consumers by what I will now call the 'virtual' consumer can be found across the board. Money in the health service went increasingly to these managerial processes, so that managers became virtual (i.e., in the stead of) patients. Other major virtual consumers were lawyers who, like audit and management, stood in the stead or on behalf of actual patients and students and threatened to sue the institutions, creating an extraordinary climate of fear. Similarly, so-called ethics committees developed whose primary purpose was to prevent litigation against the institutions.

At this point we need to look at these various fragments and see if together they represent any kind of coherent picture. Looked at as a whole, they do indeed seem to have some things in common, and surprisingly enough this is pivoted around the trope of the consumer. If audit uses terms and processes that are copied from commerce and economics, it is because the entire structure of economics is supposedly just a more efficient way of fulfilling demands that emanate originally from consumers. Competition, free trade and so forth are all supposed to make for more efficient servicing of consumer demand. A good deal of those management consultancy interventions were based on firms feeling they had lost touch with consumers and needed some outside force to help them realign their practices with consumers.

The trouble is that economists are not consumers, management consultants are not consumers, lawyers are not consumers, and managers are not consumers. They are all what might be called *virtual* consumers, who seem to have sucked authority and resources from the mass of ordinary people whom we used to regard as consumers, and used them to legitimate a huge rechannelling of resources to themselves. They are now consuming big time, but do so in the stead of real consumers. So all these trees amount to a wood we can call *virtualism* – not in the digital sense of the word 'virtual',[70] but meaning that they all stand in the stead of the real consumer.

The other principal characteristic of virtualism is that these forces do more than just displace actual consumers. They have an incredible power to change the world. So far, I have concentrated on the distance between the models used in economics and world they were supposed to model. But the reason that this matters so much is that economists have the power to change that world and seek to make it accord with their models. When an economic regime such as structural adjustment is imposed upon a country, the intention is largely to try and abolish those practices, such as currency control or welfare provision, that act as 'distortions' to the model, so that increasingly the country has to behave more and more like the economist's theoretical model of a proper market. In a way, *virtualism* is the way capitalism caught up with Marxism, which was also a theory of political economy intended to transform whole economies, to make them conform to its own idealised model of how a society should be. My arguments against textbooks in finance matter, because the people who read them then try and rewrite the world in their image.[71] Thrift[72] argues that this is partly because capitalism now knows a lot more about what it is doing, including its own performative nature. My evidence is otherwise. By examining this ethnographically, we can see that this is not an outcome of knowledge or intention, but largely the fortuitous consequence of wielding too much power. As a result much of what we observe is self-contradictory and prone to crisis, all of which makes this one of the most problematic consequences of consumption.

Value: from problem to solution[73]

Is there an alternative to virtualism? I would rather end this chapter on a positive note and suggest that there is. The most fundamental problem with all these economic theories, whether of Marxism or the market, is that they all rest upon a particular concept of value. *Mastering Finance* spends its first chapters declaring that the increase in value is in essence the very point of finance and that it will be a textbook about value. Marxist theory rests on the supposed discovery of a labour theory of value. As Marx put it,[74] 'It is not money that renders commodities commensurable. Just the contrary. It is because all commodities, as values, are realized human labour, and therefore commensurable, that their values can be measured by one and the same special commodity, and the latter be converted into the common measure of their values, i.e., into money.' McKinsey and the management consultants became missionaries who informed the world that it should recognise another ultimate form of value, *shareholder value*. And what was the name of England's largest ever audit? Best Value.

Yet they all mean different things when they use the word 'value'. So what fundamentally is value? For the epistemology of these pseudo-sciences, value needs to be an actual and consistent thing to which everything else can finally be reduced. By contrast, as an anthropologist, I make no such assumption. I would suggest we should stand back a moment and reflect on what this word 'value' does, rather than what it means. Looked at from the perspective of usage, it emerges as a really rather extraordinary and paradoxical concept. In the everyday world, value has two entirely opposite meanings. It can mean the monetary worth we ascribe to an object, as in valuing an antique piece of porcelain or a house, making it synonymous with price. Yet we also say we value our family or our religion, meaning that these are things which are irreducible to monetary evaluation. We remain blissfully unconcerned about using the same word, 'value', to mean something and simultaneously its very opposite – sometimes using both senses in adjoining sentences. But what if that's the point – that what value does is to create a bridge between value as price and value as inalienable, meaning that which cannot be priced?

This problem is central to the work of the sociologist Viviana Zelizer.[75] Her book *Pricing the Priceless Child*[76] reports the quandary of an insurance company which has to give a monetary value to the compensation to be paid out for the death of a child, who is the epitome of what we would like to regard as priceless. Recently[77] she has examined court cases where people who gave care and love, which they never wished to see monetarised, find they have to calculate a financial recompense because of arguments over inheritance or divorce. The institutions I admire are those that manage to live with this real world of value. They don't pretend to be a pseudo-science that can reduce everything to a single form of value. They work with both the qualitative and the quantitative ends of the value spectrum. I will present just two examples.

If you were to rifle through my wallet, you would find that my credit card comes from the John Lewis Partnership. John Lewis is the largest and consistently most successful chain of department stores in the UK combined with an equally successful relatively upmarket supermarket called Waitrose. During the year when I was studying shopping and also retail, I discovered that workers seemed more favourable to and identified more with this company than any other. I also found that this was the company shoppers were most positive about, an observation backed up by quantitative surveys.[78] So the company that treats its workers the best is the company that treats its customers the best. In my research the words most commonly used in relation to John Lewis were *quality* and *value*. It emerged that John Lewis does not excel at any one thing – its goods are neither the cheapest, nor the most stylish, nor the finest. Instead it represents the qualitative equivalent of an equation whose variables include function, design and price. When shoppers say that the shop is good value, they mean it has found on their behalf the ideal balance between these various qualities. It is they who have forced design and price into equivalence without privileging either. In short, the shop is credited with helping the consumers with their most important task of taking the incommensurable qualitative and quantitative factors and making them commensurable. Similarly, it was clear that shoppers trust the John Lewis shop assistants more than those in any other retail outlet to discuss their merchandise with genuine information and human empathy to their specific needs, which they perceive as directly opposed to the fake 'have a nice day' interactions they encounter in other shops. The John Lewis staff are thereby adding in another qualitative factor of considerable relevance: their personal assessment of the specific customer.

So value in John Lewis is based on the rationality of compromise where the calculation is holistic rather than reductionist, including listening to customers and giving personal advice. This is the mirror image of value as constructed in the organisation of the company itself. Most shoppers are entirely unaware of the unusual nature of the John Lewis partnership. Unlike virtually every company with which it has to compete, there is no shareholder value to John Lewis, because the company has never issued any shares. John Lewis is a partnership, where all employees are partners. It is a workers' cooperative. All profits not required for reinvestment are distributed to its workers rather than to shareholders.[79] Unlike the highly politicised socialist workers' cooperatives of the 1970s, it never pushed the idea of equality into dysfunctionality. Sales assistants are consulted but have no power to manage, which remains in the hands of professional management. John Lewis retains a slightly paternalistic aura from its foundation, but I still found that their workers were conspicuously positive about their employer. This relative lack of alienation is surly linked to the degree to which they don't just own the process, they actually own the company itself.

My second example comes from the political sphere. As was clear from this book's preface, I have been fascinated by how in the long term under social democracy Scandinavia became not only one of the wealthiest regions in the world but also the most ethical and, quite probably, the most egalitarian the world has ever known. Because I prefer actual models to theoretical or utopian ones, I also fully acknowledge the faults. Sweden has a dark history of eugenics and the region now has strong nationalist parties. My point is only that Scandinavia may be a better case than any alternative.

In his book *The Rise and Fall of the Swedish Model*,[80] Rojas reveals a social democratic system that embraced capitalism, but within a carefully designated field, retaining strict controls over its social consequences. Markets were free to innovate and invest, giving Sweden an astonishing rate of growth. But they were not allowed to dilute a commitment to equality, there being relatively little differentiation of income between employer and the employed. Visitors came to envy the provision of child care, the accessibility of medical care and, above all, the lack of any major underclass of mass poverty. The case refutes by example the insistence in the US and the UK that economic success requires competition fostered by large pay differentials.

I have suggested that all institutions tend eventually to their own self-aggrandisement. According to Rojas, the very success of the Swedish model led to a reification of ideology which unbalanced this compromise. By 1993, state spending had risen to 74 per cent of GDP, and government became increasingly bureaucratic and mistook relative equality for absolute homogeneity. The social democrats lost power and the country become more like others, though there remains a distinctive egalitarianism to Scandinavia more generally. But this decline should not detract from what we can learn from its longevity, having been established in 1932, and success. If value can remain a balance between quantity and quality, money and the inalienable, profits and people, it is possible to have both wealth and welfare.

The other factor that led to the decline of this regional alternative has been the overwhelming power of global financial structures, based on virtualism, that try to make all countries accord with the models of academic economics. The premise of efficiency, used to justify this encroachment, remains false. US workers work about a third as much again to earn the same amount as Scandinavian workers and receive far less welfare provision. I believe social democracy remains viable. It is simply not fashionable, and even its citation as a historical precedent seems to have been suppressed by the dominant axioms of economics.

I really don't think I can be accused of selecting utopian or unfeasible examples for my alternative political economy. I picked one of the most consistently successful and profitable companies in the UK and one of the most successful and wealthy regional economies in the world. So I would hope it has been clear what this chapter is for and not just what it is against.[81] We may seem to have strayed far from a direct encounter with consumers and consumption, but much of what I call virtualism takes its legitimacy from its pretence that it represents a new orientation to consumers. This needs to be challenged, since actually it represents the replacement of real consumers with the virtual. By contrast, my alternative theory of value, which I believe lies behind the success of John Lewis and Scandinavian social democracy, accepts the need for a qualitative engagement with the specifics of actual people and their welfare concerns while protecting the anonymity of bureaucracy. Indeed, there is a natural fit between anthropological ideals of holism and empathy and the detailed and patient articulation that comes with constant grounding in ethnography that could or should lead to these aspirations for a political economy, based on the colloquial use of the word 'value'.[82]

To conclude, this book is clearly no more anti-business than it is anti-consumption. It has on many occasions acknowledged the contribution of commercial enterprise to the reduction of poverty and the increase of welfare. It has defended the role of consumption, on the same grounds, and respected people's demands for goods rather than dismissing them as signs that they are deluded, stupid or merely fooled by advertising. At the same time it is remarkable that, even following a vast financial crisis, where the prime culprit seems to have been a financial system that retained close links with idealised academic models of economics and thereby lost almost all contact with a more grounded world, we see almost no serious attempts to challenge or curb that system. The interests of the financial system remain privileged over the interests of those it was supposed to serve, including the interests of ordinary commerce.

One reason is that there seems to be no prospect of rethinking the way economics is taught as an academic subject. There could be an education in real-world political economy that used examples such as Scandinavia and John Lewis, the evident contradictions of pension-fund capitalism and fashion-based consultancy, whose focus was on the consequences for welfare and the planet. There could be an education which focuses on examples of how to use economic instruments for securing the welfare of populations and ethical ends rather than economics as a theoretical and increasingly autonomous structure in which means supplant the ends. However, as long as economics remains dominated by models which strive to be socially decontextualised and ignorant of qualitative research, it will create systems that are antithetical to people's welfare.

6

How Not to Save a Planet

GRACE: Hi, come on in, you're very welcome.

MIKE: Thank you. Oh, that's a rather magnificent animal. Looks like pure tabby. Is she pregnant?

GRACE: No, just ridiculously fat. Her colouring is quite something though, isn't it? She's getting on a bit these days, so that's mostly where you will see her, sleeping in the corner.

MIKE: Well, it's great to see you both again. I really enjoyed our earlier chat, and it has set me thinking – though I guess today is going to be a whole lot more difficult. We can't just witter on, giving our opinions on consumption and the world at large. We promised we would end up with something concrete by way of solutions.

GRACE: In the meantime, I assume we all read Danny Miller's latest. So what did you think of it?

MIKE: Er, not much. There was nothing about the environment.

CHRIS: Me neither. I think he should just have called it *More Stuff*.

MIKE: Or *Stuff and Nonsense*?

GRACE: Oh Lawd! That's what you get for asking two male academics about the work of another male academic. OK, to be honest I didn't get much out of it either, but that's because I teach his stuff extensively and, as he makes clear, it is essentially a summary of work he has already published. I had hoped for more or better jokes, though. Oh well...

MIKE: Actually, I have been doing more than reading books. One of the reasons I was very keen to have this debate today is that I have been hatching a plot. I think I have got *the* solution in hand and I was getting desperate to share it with you too. In essence my problem is this. I know we can sit here and debate and enjoy ourselves, but at the same time we are aware that as social scientists we will have almost no impact upon anything or anyone.

CHRIS: That's going a bit far.

MIKE: Come on – when was the last time anyone took a blind bit of notice of a bunch of academics, unless they are economists or scientists? This is England, not Europe. In this country they listen to footballers' wives before they listen to the likes of us. So let's be realistic for a moment. Is there anything that we as academics might hope to achieve here? And I am thinking that there is perhaps just one constituency that might be open to academic initiatives and that is the world of education itself. If we are going to have an impact then we need to transform consciousness so that all consumption becomes resonant with its origins and its consequences. And that really is a matter of education, which is what we three are actually involved with.

So I think we should start by asking some simple questions about the basic school curriculum.[1] I simply can't work out why we teach what we teach. There is nothing wrong with schoolchildren learning chemical formulae or about the Romans. But how much will this knowledge be used by them as adults? By contrast, they know nothing about the stuff they actually live with. Half my students couldn't tell you how weaving works, let alone metalwork or plastics, and it's getting worse. As Miller noted at the end of his book, what is trickling down to schools are those preposterous formulae of theoretical economics that just delude the world. Soon they will be able to spout rational choice theory while having none of the knowledge they need to make rational choices. Above all, they can't be expected to change consumption when they leave school with so little knowledge about its origins and a sense of the people who actually make these goods as well as the consequences of consumption.

CHRIS: I remember at my school we had this video of smiling cocoa plantation workers followed by the arrival of the cocoa by ship to Britain, where it was turned into bars of chocolate. I vaguely remember desperately wanting to eat more chocolate, while being none the wiser about the implications for producers. But today isn't there actually quite a lot of good stuff around on these topics sponsored by Oxfam and others?

MIKE: Certainly, but this should be at the core of education, not just an add-on. Also I think there are ways we can make this much, much more effective. Let me give you a few. What I think children respond to are good stories that concern them directly as individuals. So you want to present consumption as the full story, not just the plantation work or mineral extraction and then the miraculous appearance of the finished product. They need all the in-between stages: the shipping and the processing, but also the retail buyers, people in management and quality control. But the real clincher would be if these are the stories of goods that they are subsequently going to consume. The goods should be produced and labelled with the names of these schoolchildren or, if that is impractical, at least the name of the school.

GRACE: I'm sorry, I've lost the plot of your story. How would that work, the logistics?

MIKE: Imagine every school linked by webcam to the producers of just three quite ordinary goods. The first is a simple product, such as a banana. Each week they webcam to a stage in its progress – a farmer applying pesticide, the shipping, the ripening sheds in

Portsmouth. But this is a banana from a plantation which is being grown for that particular destination – say, the primary school of St Mary of Nortun on Sea. Then take a second, more complex product – for example, a bottle of ginger beer. Again the company has agreed to label each bottle with the name of the school, so they are watching the process behind 'their' ginger beer that eventually they will drink. Such 'bespoke' bottles will need to be a bit more expensive, but on this scale not that much more. So then with weekly webcam they follow the production of ginger, of sugar, of the industrial waste processes that produce the gas, the glass bottling and all the rest of it. Secondary schoolchildren can realise that farmers have opinions on the IMF or the European policy on biofuels, and that workers talk about regulation and liberalisation. They can audit each stage for issues of energy, carbon footprints and other environmental issues, as well as fairness and welfare. Above all, they can see that every time they make a consumer choice it has consequences, not just the green consumption but for all manner of issues.

My third product would be local, from a place they can imagine their parents working in or eventually working in themselves. And the idea should work in reverse. After all, kids in the Caribbean end up eating Cadburys, since the cocoa is refined here, not there, and those schoolchildren should see what we do to their cocoa. So, take Miller's discussion of blue jeans and let children see the issues around thirsty cotton and the treatments that make the jeans look worn.[2] Ideally I would then follow this through to when they throw away the empty ginger beer bottles and look at the phase of waste, since waste is often the start of a whole new cycle, and one of the key consequences of consumption is waste itself.[3] So basically my idea is that we place consumption and its consequences right at the heart of what we mean by the very word 'education'. Let them learn about something they actually do and which has consequences, so that they would actually be educated.

GRACE: Gosh, that's a fantastic proposal, Mike. I love your idealism. I feel terrible saying anything other than, yes, let's do it. But, to be honest, I really think that perhaps you are jumping the gun a bit here. I was looking forward to today because I strongly feel that we need to have a much more extended discussion of the wider issues and potential solutions. That might then give us a sense of where such a scheme fits in, and what difference it might actually make, not to mention its feasibility.

MIKE: Hmmm, you sound somewhat underwhelmed. Would you really just dismiss this? I have spoken to several people responsible for the geography curriculum in schools. It might work, you know.

GRACE: I'm not dismissing it: I promise we will come back to it. I really don't want to close this off at all. It's just I think we need to see what it looks like after we have had a wider discussion. It may then appear still more attractive. But let's just see how things go. Is that OK?

(Changing the subject) As it happens, we haven't been idle, either. We spent the time visiting one of my PhD students, Tom McDonald,[4] in China. While everyone else goes either to Shanghai and Beijing or to some traditional rural village, I get my students to search for a kind of middling ordinariness. Tom is based in the kind of small town no one has any reason to study. But the place was amazing. It's like Le Corbusier was an infection rather than an architect: a plague of tower blocks with tens of thousands of brand new apartments; streets of shops selling stone floor tiles, plastic furniture, bathroom and kitchen units; wide roads and new glitzy glass-fronted bus stations, with hardly any traffic...as yet. They are clearly building infrastructure for just that massive increase in consumption I was talking about in our last meeting, and that my Filipino relations would sell their souls for. When the

CHRIS:

MIKE:

GRACE:

MIKE:

older Chinese realised I had 'tasted bitterness' – that is, been born into poverty – they just assumed I would celebrate all this as manifest happiness.

CHRIS: Just until they get their housing bubble crisis, which, believe me, is coming some time soon. And I am really *not* one of those who would celebrate a crash as though it were some kind of nemesis from nature. If I am consistent with regard to one thing, then it is with poverty.

MIKE: Fine and good. But if you had gone to Beijing you would have seen traffic jams and smog of equally legendary proportions, though they are now taking some action.[5] But I really don't want to start from places such as India or China, because I am fed up to the back teeth with friends in London who seem to be blaming the Chinese for climate change, when all the indices show that we are the villains in this story. In per capita terms they remain way behind us in problem creation. But also we really don't want to repeat our last meeting. It just doesn't matter where consumption is increasing because, when it comes to the planet, the regions where climate change has an impact may be entirely unrelated to the regions that have caused it. This really is a planetary problem.

OK, I can see you are not totally convinced by my educational plans, so let me start at the other end and address some of those issues of the wider context. If Chris is fixated on poverty, then I am fixated on something else, something called the Fifth Assessment of the Intergovernmental Panel on Climate Change, which is due to report in 2014. It's a bit of a mouthful, I know, but it's what everyone should be keeping their eye on. In our last meeting I brought up Hulme and the uncertainties around climate change, but they are pretty serious academics.

GRACE: A mite too serious?

MIKE: Not on this topic. Anyway, if you won't accept my other plans, then I am bloody well sticking with serious – in fact, sticking with boring, tedious science.

After all, it's not like we would accept climate change because we had a nasty winter or read about a flood somewhere. Real climate scientists do the dull stuff, aggregate data based on thousands of observations in many different circumstances. And we have the maturity to work with probabilities. Each subsequent scientific report on climate change[6] gives us more authoritative data, even if they consist of even more variable information about the causes, nature, extent and potential consequences of climate change. In particular, there is now consensus that, even if good measures are put in place today, there are already serious problems as a result of human activities that cannot now be undone or at least may take, in some cases, a millennium to restore fully.

So, Grace, it's not like I would dispute your vista of inevitable and vast increases in consumption. It just reinforces my feeling that we must, must, must act quickly with regard to these issues, and not put our heads in the sand. I am getting older, and I feel I just can't bear to be the generation that knew that we were screwing things up for the future generations and failed to act. After all, I have known about this for a very long time. As I mentioned at our last meeting, I go way back to a raising of consciousness that came with the 1972 Club of Rome report,[7] which for environmentalists is a bit like saying I saw The Beatles. We all know the figures of 600 million people potentially inundated by sea-level rises. And it's not just climate change. That first green agenda had much more to do with natural resources being exploited to extinction. Those problems have not gone away. Then came all those concerns with toxicity and fears of disease – the evidence that global farming and trade might lead to global epidemics. I get just as scared by those threats from bird flu as from climate change. Global farming stays on my agenda for many reasons.

But, having been part of the doomsaying for so long, I have absolutely no desire to appear as some latter-day prophet striding up and down Oxford Street with my placard telling people that the end of the world is nigh. So, yes, simply banging on and on about critique becomes just one more form of self-indulgence. The point is to face up to these apparently irreconcilable truths. Somehow we have both to increase and decrease consumption dramatically at the very same time. We don't have time for the utopian green ideals any more. I just want to find something that might work, something feasible. That seems to be our job today, eminently feasible alternatives. We don't get to leave until we have got to that point. OK?

CHRIS: OK. Well, since Grace forced us into reading Miller, we might as well try and start from where he leaves off. On the one hand, I was pleasantly surprised that, for a book that was focused on consumption, he still managed a final chapter that was pretty unequivocal in its critique of economics. On the other hand, I found that chapter exceptionally naïve, especially when he seems to dismiss the idea that there is any kind of 'cabal' driving the contemporary political economy. What about Monbiot's[8] excavation of the power of commercial lobby groups on the creation of the US Tea Party? This whole thing is just a lot more intelligent and directed than he is willing to concede. Worse than that, I read Miller's chapters and I see nothing about the consequences of consumption I most care about, the exploitation and the oppression. What kind of anthropologist is it that leaves out the suffering of people? You don't do that, Grace. When we go shopping for clothes you are always giving me a mini-lecture on how the trend towards fast fashion and the ridiculously low prices at supermarkets and Primark are directly linked to appalling conditions among workers in Bangladesh,[9] where people who were once tailors now just endlessly sew sequins into the night. That's a literally 'down the line' connection of economic cause and consequence. Why isn't Miller telling that story?

GRACE: Oh, come on, Chris, we have been through this a million times. Anthropologists, including Miller, have constantly drawn attention to the linkages down the commodity chain from product back to production. He teaches about ethical fashion and the implications for workers. Remember, it was Danny who told us about that new work on the impact of bauxite extraction on indigenous peoples in India. But, however much we raise consciousness about the impact on workers, we fail to make headway on changing these circumstances because we simply misunderstand the nature of consumption itself. He wants to finish sorting out the equation by explaining the factor we kept getting wrong, and replacing unfeasible ideals with – to use Mike's phrase – feasible solutions.

CHRIS: I'm sorry, but, without evoking that experience of suffering, this to me is just another portrait of consumption without a heart. Anyway, when it comes to the actual nature of market capitalism, I think it's Miller that's wrong. He really ought to keep up with writers like David Harvey[10] who have spent years showing that there is both a logic and a directive behind privatisation and securitisation and the rest of the neo-liberal agenda, with a long history which is not just compatible with the study of financial crises but the cause. I am not going to give vent to my own theories, which are based on Harvey, since I can't see either of you accepting my stance.

But this does matter for the issues raised by Mike. Because the other point that I think Miller misses is that there is a consequence to the market which you will find in other writers such as Tim Jackson.[11] What I still want to call capitalism, because that word transcends Miller's insistence on its internal inconsistency, seems to me a self-perpetuating mechanism that works with only two gears, either continual increase and expansion or crisis reverse. Whoever built the market vehicle just forgot to supply the gearbox with a slot for neutral. That's why those of us interested in sustainability keep pointing the finger at capitalism as such a significant part of the problem. Markets can't cope with the ideas of sufficiency or even satisfaction; they are relentlessly expansive by their very nature. So, to my mind, there are two clear problems here. Sure, one is consumption and the reasons why people want goods, but to me there remains an equally intransigent problem of the market itself as a system.

GRACE: That's it, that's exactly it! That's exactly what makes me angry beyond belief when it comes to this issue of proffered solutions to climate change. When I listen to these so-called solutions, honestly, it makes me want to explode!

MIKE: Well, before you do, I think I should say that I am also getting a bit worried. To be honest, Grace, of course I am all ears; this is the stuff I live. We have been lurching from Kyoto to Copenhagen to appearing currently to be stuck in the rough. So, please don't just dismiss all this work. A lot of friends of mine are involved in the intricacies of such discussions, and they include many sincere, conscientious people.

GRACE: Yes but...

MIKE: No, honestly, it's not just glib activists performing the rites of nature in front of journalists. Many of my friends are serious activists for reasons you would certainly respect. They do the research and the long labour that goes before and around such meetings. And it's based on a real concern for the evidence and every thought for the consequences.

GRACE: Mike, you don't even know what I'm going to say. It really has nothing to do with activists, good or bad; those are not the people I was about to attack. I have bigger fish to fry.

MIKE: OK, sorry, I do get a bit touchy about the way we greens are portrayed these days. And, to be honest, our last meeting didn't really help. But, fine, say your piece and I will wait my turn.

GRACE: Don't worry, I am entirely used to Chris, who inevitably looks like he is tongue-biting the moment other people try and get a word in.

CHRIS: Excuse me: I have been very, very restrained. I had hardly started before I let myself be interrupted.

GRACE: I had noticed, and I am honestly impressed. But it was what you said about markets and consumption that concerns me right now. As it happens, Mike, I don't think for one moment that the problem with the likes of Kyoto and Copenhagen has anything to do with activists or greens of any complexion. I admire that kind of activism and feel guilty for my own lack of it. Quite the opposite: the problem as I see it is at the other end. It is with the people who *do* have the power and who *are* determining the proffered solutions at the present time. It's not even as though nothing has happened as a result of these conferences. There are of course all those targets that are mainly being missed, but there is something quite extraordinary in, for example, the deliberate and systematic invention of an entirely new market – the market for carbon. It's quite something just to invent a whole new market and set it in motion.[12] That's what makes Chris's point against Miller, that even when it comes to solutions we are still talking about markets.

As far as I can tell – and I know that, Mike, you have much more expertise than I do – there are really two main trends that are emerging as proffered solutions to these issues of climate change. The first is precisely this new market in carbon emissions, so that it becomes expensive in a new way actually to create additional carbon. And, as I understand it, there are also possible markets in other pollutants, such as sulphur dioxide and nitrogen oxides. The other pretty obvious trend is towards more and more green consumer products. I guess these started as fringe alternatives, but today they are dominated by supermarket products – not that this is a bad thing if we want them to have a serious impact.

I guess most people today want to feel they have some stake in doing their bit for the environment through buying at least a few organic or ecologically less destructive goods. And in response to this there is an ever growing field of possibilities for consumers who want to go green, to choose more sustainable, more earth-friendly consumer goods. In this respect, the protestors seem to be on the same side as the politicians. We are supposed to favour electric cars over petrol ones, and then biofuels over oil. The politicians collude in this. So we even subsidise biofuels to try and get people to favour them, despite evidence for their lack of true green credentials when made from non-tropical agricultural products. We have this vision that people can learn to love green goods because those goods are expressing their love and concern for future generations.

So what's my problem? Why I am not celebrating the rise of carbon markets and of eco-goods with a nice glass of organic Chardonnay? Oh, sorry, Mike, I promised to ease off on the stereotyping. And actually at this point I really do want to get serious, because this is exactly what makes me angry. I mean, think about what I have just described for one minute. What are the two dominant solutions that are currently on offer with respect to climate change? Solution number one is a new range of markets and solution number two is an increase in consumer choice that includes green products. And yet, five minutes ago, what did Chris describe as the two main sources of the problem, the two forces which have created the problem of climate change? One was the nature of the market and the other was the nature of expanding consumption. These are precisely the forces that by their very nature lead to an inexorable increase in demand.

I won't actually rage, but in my very, very best Homer Simpson accent – *d'oh*! How unbelievably stupid can we be? The only two solutions on offer are exactly the two things that are creating the problem in the first place. Climate change is a result of the impact of markets and consumer choice, and yet the only two solutions we are being offered are more markets and more consumer choice. Is there really nothing in the deep pools of global imagination left except these two? Have they devoured all the other fish so that they are the only things left that rise to our baits?

MIKE: Only too true, but very confusing. Since I know you are fond of Miller, I can't imagine you see this as some huge conspiracy theory, and you have been defending consumption. So how do you figure we end up at this point? Plus I am not entirely sure why you see this as unbelievably stupid. It's not that uncommon to use the instruments that cause problems as the means to their solutions.

GRACE: Well, let's start with the first question. How come? That's not hard at all, because at the end of the day the people who have power, the people who can pursue governments and industries to take one direction rather than another, are definitely not the activists. They are almost always these days going to be economists. Economists seem to be the only people anyone listens to these days, unless it's the psychologists, who, as Miller argued, sleep in the same epistemological bed. And, as long as it's economists who are writing the lyrics, everyone will remain singing from the same old hymn sheet – praises and hallelujahs to markets and consumer choice. I honestly don't think they *can* come up with anything else. Yes, before you say anything, I know it's not all economists – the Keynesians would be different. So, when I say economists, then like Miller I always mean the dominant lot, not the dominated lot. So as far as I am concerned there is a perfectly simple and plausible explanation as to how come there is no difference at all between the problems and the solutions.

Which leads to the second of Mike's questions and, I agree, the more important one. It would be OK if there was some reason to think these solutions could work. But they just can't and won't. I want to start from the same place as you, Mike. So, in preparation for this meeting, I re-read the Stern Report, and, sure, it may well be about the best of what we've got when it comes to trying to mobilise political muscle behind addressing the issue of climate change. But it's still called *The Economics of Climate Change*[13] because, for all its virtues, it's also a prime example of what I am talking about. It remains irredeemably economistic with all those incredible biases. Things will only ever work thanks to better markets and incentives, not just carbon markets,[14] but emission reduction also needs to be a market.[15] Indeed, it seems like the solution is always to make a better market. Like where he says – excuse the notes – 'lack of certainty over the future pricing of the carbon externality will reduce the incentive to innovate',[16] or where he states that the research and development should be overwhelmingly in the private sector.[17] For Stern, the main purpose of regulation is to help produce and build markets.[18] The weird thing is that, as MacKenzie showed, creating a new carbon market actually had nothing to do with the private sector; it's an initiative that came from government policy. Yet the obvious roles of politics and government in the areas we inhabit, such as research, are constantly belittled. Even the section on ethics seems to have been smuggled in only by making it replete with absurd algebraic equations,[19] so that ethics comes dressed up as economic formulae.

Stern only really allows governments to play a role when it comes to his final section on 'adaption' – that is, how we deal with the potentially devastating consequences of a climate change we have been unable to prevent – though that does suggest some welcome realism. But this is in essence the typical economist's notion that governments exist mainly to clear up the mess and the failure of markets. At least he is not one of those economists who would probably now see floods and famine largely as market opportunities or stimuli to innovation. So, while Stern helps to focus on the problems, he retains all the bias of an economist, which also means he blithely ignores the central role of markets in pretty much every economic crisis we have ever had, because all his solutions have to come through markets.

MIKE: It's funny that you pick on Stern. I do just the same thing. You know academics tend to be a bit like theologians. We are always harshest with the heretics, the ones who share most of our beliefs but then deviate, rather than keeping our invective for the real bastards. Yes, Stern is an economist, and he does illustrate the problems we have with economists, but why pick on him as against the unreconstructed climate change deniers? As you admitted, at least you always feel with Stern that he has a heart and it's clearly linked to his brain. My recollection is that this is also a report with lots of small sensible suggestions – for example, the beneficial side effect of moving aluminium smelting to Iceland.[20] He understands that the core priorities should concern places with massive low-lying populations, such as Bangladesh, and he does at least try to integrate welfare ethics and see climate as something bigger than just one more externality. He is on our side. So doesn't it seem to be just a little churlish to start by attacking our friends rather than our real enemies?

CHRIS: Actually, I think both of you have really rather strayed from the point that I know Grace initially intended to make. You can't be married to someone without after a while being able to talk their talk. I really don't think our issue is the virtues and vices of economists. The point, surely, was that all of this might be justified if carbon markets actually worked in terms of helping us deal with climate change. As Mike pointed out at the beginning, this is all just too important for that. Is the creation of a market in carbon, or anything else, going to benefit the planet substantially? That's the question, and, since we have discussed it at some length, I know that both Grace and myself are equally clear that the answer is no.

In fact, carbon markets are rather like economists to the degree that they overly simplify complex issues and overly obfuscate simple issues. After all, what does a carbon market actually do? You trade permits for using carbon. So you make it look as though the developed world is cutting back by trading the rights to pollute to the developing world. This is not a terribly hard thing to accomplish because these days a place like the UK is less invested in manufacturing. So we can easily appear to be creating less carbon. The only catch is that mass of carbon which has been used to make the goods that are then traded back in and actually consumed by those very same developed countries that initially traded out those carbon vouchers. Officially the EU cut carbon emissions by 6 per cent between 1990 and 2008, until you take into account that, 'Overall, the rich world's increase in "carbon imports" is six times bigger than cuts in the developed world's own carbon emissions.'[21] The carbon just boomerangs back in, in the form of finished goods that now contain within themselves the energy used in their production. This is quite apart from the ease by which countries can fake the accounts so that in a very short time huge amounts of carbon appear to have gone missing.[22] In the end, the only thing actually being traded in this so-called carbon market is really just blame. Everyone can now more easily blame someone else. Once again, so far from being models of efficiency, markets turn out to be utterly inefficient and ineffective instruments for actually doing something. A carbon market doesn't help us with climate change; it just makes climate change problems look like something familiar to economists. It's another example of what Miller called virtualism. But, in providing the illusion of acting on the problem, they are really doing us far more harm than good.

GRACE: OK, so we are starting to get somewhere. We agree that carbon markets are a fake and largely reinforce our collective assumption that putting economists in charge of finding solutions to climate change is like hiring a wolf to find out why we keep losing sheep. But, to go back to Mike's confusion, I was the one stridently defending consumption in our first conversation, so I feel I should also be the one to put the boot into the second of the currently proffered solutions, the role of consumers when it comes to climate change issues. Because I think in some ways appealing to consumers is even more pernicious than appealing to markets. And this is precisely the area where I think we do need to take Miller's own research on board. Remember his ethnographic discussion at the end of his chapter on shopping – all those contradictions in ethical shopping and how consumers convince themselves that they are doing good in their shopping choices, when actually they are motivated largely by their own self-interest.

Well, to be honest, I felt that Miller's ethnography as it specifically relates to this issue is pretty thin, but I was recently sent an excellent PhD thesis by a US anthropology student, Cindy Isenhour,[23] who carried out an ethnographic study of what you might call 'best practice' consumers. These are relatively well-off Swedish consumers with a genuine concern to promote sustainability through their consumer choices. She has far more robust evidence to make very similar points – wonderful ethnographic reportage about how consumers conceptualise nature, the different ways in which they legitimate their own consumption choices, and the various forms of status that can be gained by looking green. In practice, 'the defence of consumer choice can thus be seen as a defence of power and privilege'.[24] This is backed up still further by the recent book by Norgaard.[25] We have all agreed that the Norwegians are our best out of the currently existing societies, and Norgaard's ethnography is of Bygdaby. This is a small rural town that seems like the perfect community, with high levels of political involvement, considerable awareness of green issues, and a strong and justifiable claim to virtue and ethics. Yet, even here, they actually largely ignore that green knowledge in practice. The topic gets neatly shunted into the general area of small talk, since climate change is, after all, about the weather, and the weather was always the mainstay of small talk. But all this talk has very little actual impact, apart from increasing people's sense of guilt, which Scandinavians in general are pretty good at.

Scandinavia remains prime territory for explicitly showing concern for nature, combined with a state-led emphasis on rational modernism as a basis for sustainable strategies. So you would think it would make the perfect region to kick-start green consumption. But what Isenhour and Norgaard make clear is that the economists' logic of putting the emphasis back on consumer choice – even these ideal citizen-consumers – does precious little in relation to the big structural issues that will actually have any sort of significant impact upon the planet. We have speculated for ages that, if we switched to greener electric cars, the environmental benefits would be cancelled out, since people would just drive more. The evidence is now there, because the Swedes have switched to hybrid cars and, yes, as a result they do now drive more than they used to, and, yes, their transport system is now emitting more greenhouse gases than before the switch,[26] pretty much exactly matching Monbiot's[27] scepticism about such solutions.

MIKE: As you clearly noticed when you came to visit, I am big on eco- and green products. But these days you are certainly aware that the markets are only too willing to get involved in 'greenwashing'[28] their products, which is done mainly to make the companies look good. When I am shopping I sometimes think that the more polluting the company, the bigger the green advertising budgets, thus the plethora of green goods, which drives me nuts.

GRACE: I sympathise, but the bigger picture here is that green consumption is seen as the right and proper way to solve climate change, simply because economists will inevitably want to cede any actual moral authority to consumer choice. It's pretty much the only authority they ever recognise, and even that is often only in theory.[29] But, for all the reasons you have given us, climate change is way too important to become a matter of consumer choice. You just can't leave the future of the planet to depend on whether consumers think it's higher or lower status to be seen with supermarket plastic bags or recycling boxes outside of their homes. As Isenhour points out, housewives, who are generally also in employment as well as responsible for their families, are already landed with enough responsibilities without being expected to save the planet somewhere between child care and washing up. I say that with some feeling...

MIKE: Well, I certainly agree that climate change can't be a consumer luxury. And you are right, there is evidence that, when things are good, people prioritise green goods and listen to Al Gore, and then, when recession bites, they decide to have other priorities. The politicians, who were busy embracing green views at one moment, can see it's no longer an electoral winner and turn to other issues instead. Do you remember Cameron's claims to be the green candidate before the last UK election? What happened to all that?

GRACE: Far be it from me to defend David Cameron, but you know we constantly blame politicians, and you have just shown why that's shallow. Politicians have to follow the public or they don't get re-elected. The real problem, then, is that in recession climate change is no longer a public priority which drives the change in politics. But, at the end of the day, climate change is either happening or it isn't happening. Its existence isn't at the whim of consumer concern or citizens' votes, and therefore it can't be at the whim of politics that depends on those votes either.

MIKE: Gosh, I guess about the most radical thing one can do these days is actually to defend politicians!

GRACE: I would actually, at least compared to my lot back home. But my real point is that some things transcend democratic ideals. Recall Miller discussing his ethnography of audit, when citizens are asked whether to prioritise the mayor's plan for transport or dog-poo on the street. Making everything depend upon votes means losing the authority of professionals. You can't expect or presume that all consumers are going to read the Stern Report or Mike's supersized science report. Frankly, even if far more consumers made green choices in their shopping, the impact on climate change would be marginal. Supermarket bags and recycling boxes are really sops to help consumers think they are being good and involved citizens, but that is not where the action really needs to be right now. I know some academics like Anthony Giddens[30] have argued that it's partly that people don't see the immediate impact, otherwise they would respond. But then Giddens hasn't worked with consumers. None of the people who have researched actual consumers, whether Miller, Isenhour or Norgaard, support that conjecture. The problem is that everyone has their own idea of what consumption is or what they want consumers to be. The economists want them to act in a particular way to stimulate the economy, the greens in another way to curb the economy. But this is all a projection: none of it comes from scholarship about what consumption actually is.

MIKE: I admit that what I found refreshing in Miller was when he wasn't trying to make consumption into this or into that, in order to serve some agenda, but rather just trying to observe it closely and work out what it actually is.

GRACE: And what does he conclude? At one level most consumption is either about basic household provisioning, as in food and clothing, or what Sen[31] would call increasing one's capabilities in the world. More deeply, it is also about the intensity of relationships with the people you care most about or live with, about status and local symbolic systems that relate to Christmas or thrift, or class relations in France or ethnic relations in Trinidad. Consumption will continue to be about these things, and that will always trump attempts to make it into something else. The problem with trying to make consumption about saving the planet is most fully evident in Miller's discussion of Linda Snell from the radio series *The Archers*.

MIKE: OK, I'd better confess here to a secret vice: I actually listened to *The Archers* for about ten years. It used it to give me a fifteen-minute break from my kids, who were trained never to interrupt me during this little 'sacred' period – though I think that has more to do with the unremitting nature of parenting small children than with any addiction to soaps.

GRACE: Oh, don't apologise. You should see Chris and anything that suggests we might miss *EastEnders*. But the point about Linda Snell is that a person who goes on about the big issues like climate change and world ethics doesn't thereby come across as warm; instead they seem cold and distant. That is because everyday consumption is largely about your nearest and dearest, about being thoughtful to your grandmother or your lover. If consumption really was all materialistic greed, then the issue of climate change would be heaps easier. This is even truer for the rest of the world. I know I have probably bored you with the issue of Filipino aspirations. But I was recently reading Wilhite's[32] research on rising consumption and its environmental consequences in Kerala in South India. It's exactly what you would expect: a combination of local forces, such as dowry inflation, with global forces, such as migration to the Gulf states, leads to a rise in expectations that normalise high energy consumption through installing air conditioning or buying cars, while the ideals of frugality, which had been embedded in religion, are increasingly displaced by aspirations to an affluence the potentiality of which is revealed by television. So we have the full spectrum, from peasants in India to the elite of Sweden, and it all comes to the same conclusion. The planet is no more going to be saved by green consumption than by flying pigs. So, to conclude – yes, I am outraged by the fact that the only solutions to an overconsumption which derives from the relationship between

	market supply and consumer demand is yet another market and yet more consumer choice. And, yes, Chris, it's not just because it shows the banality of economists; it's because they manifestly don't work as solutions, and, as Mike keeps pointing out, that matters.
MIKE:	Oh, well, I have to say I am more than a little surprised. I was convinced you were going to take the opposite view and accuse me of ignoring the proper authority of consumers. It's one of the reasons I wanted to start the debate with consumer education. Given that you share Miller's obsession with consumers, I would never have predicted that you would see them as largely irrelevant to planet saving. It's funny, because I'm your classic green consumer. I carefully inspect and agonise over nearly everything I buy. But, now I think about it, I won't assume your arguments detract from those acts of personal responsibility. I am sure you agree we each should aim green. And I do want to get back to my scheme at some point.
GRACE:	Absolutely.
MIKE:	OK. Well, if you grant me that, then I guess I can concede in turn that we can't leave the future of the planet to the degree to which consumers accept that responsibility. Unfortunately, what you say is only too true. So, at this point, it seems that we really do seem to agree on the negatives. But, just to remind you, given today's agenda, all your criticisms still constitute what we called the easy bit. So now I assume that has to be our point of departure. I clearly have to nail my colours to the mast by providing some alternative solution somewhere that will work in the short term. And I recognise my consumer education ideas are more long term.
GRACE:	Oh, good. I was rather hoping that this would be the point when Mike takes the floor. No offence: you probably wouldn't have invited this debate if you hadn't been storing up yet more private schemes of the planet-saving variety. As it happens, I readily admit I am in the uncomfortable position of feeling

more assured about what I think won't work or can't happen. I get a bit hazier when it comes to alternative positive and concrete proposals, although I know we agreed that that would be the priority.

MIKE: Oh, don't apologise. My soap box was all ready, waiting in the wings. Though let's be clear on what we are and are not trying to do here. I know earlier on I was trying to add in all those things we really should be considering alongside that of climate change. But perhaps we can be a little modest.

GRACE: What, with my husband? You must be joking.

CHRIS: Now...

MIKE: Look, none of us is exactly what you would call reticent. But my point is that it's bad enough three of us pontificating at this level without deluding ourselves into thinking we are going to resolve every relevant issue. In fact, Grace, you have only deepened the conundrum. We have all got together because we all teach consumption, but you refuse to acknowledge that consumption should be curbed, and you have just argued that green consumption doesn't do a whole lot either. So what's left? I figure that what we can do is try and use what we now know about consumption to differentiate the legitimate and the justified from the illegitimate and the destructive in order to ensure that there is still a planet around to be consumed. Let's stick to what we know and leave the other issues to other expertise.

CHRIS (looking across at Grace, who nods): Yes, that was pretty much both Grace's and my understanding of the collective brief, if the agenda for three academics having a discussion could ever be called a 'brief'.

MIKE: OK, then, I would start from the kind of interest you got a glimpse of when Chris found me in the state of rapture I seem to fall into with every copy of *The Economist*'s *Technology Quarterly*, bringing forth my inner geek. There are countless climate change books which want to argue that the way to resolve the problems of old technologies is with new technologies, varying from the possibilities of saltwater agriculture to algae biofuels.[33] Some of them are sort of science-fiction scenarios of space umbrellas protecting us from the sun. But there is plenty of more solid stuff. For example, I recently read Bjørn Lomborg's *Smart Solutions to Climate Change*. There was a lovely paper on something called 'black carbon migration',[34] which linked to another of my favourite genres, best described as romantic tales of alternative technologies. In this instance it turns out that some Californian ex-hippies are creating the perfect stoves for people still using firewood and the like in rural areas.[35] Apparently one of the key problems for climate change is not some new-fangled industrial complex but the soot that arises from cooking with wood by those who can't afford anything else. Thanks to population increase, this retains a huge impact. I would have thought this should appeal to you, Grace, since it seems to takes us back into anthropology, which I assume shades into development studies.

GRACE: You should know academics better than that, Mike. Anthropology and development studies certainly share terrain, and the predictable result is that most of the time they absolutely can't stand each other.

MIKE: Well, that's a pity, since some interdisciplinary work would really help right now. For example, one of my personal ambitions is to establish a Centre for Digital Sustainability. So far, the words 'digital sustainability' have meant how to sustain digital formats, but I want to turn this around and link my teaching on digital culture with that on environmentalism. Rather than assume that all new technologies simply add to the problem of climate change, it's pretty obvious that digital technologies can lead in the opposite direction. We now have music without the manufacturing, photography without the chemicals. My centre would examine the entire gamut of ways in which digital culture could be used systematically to replace unsustainable material cultures while actually retaining the social benefits. And this should appeal to you, Chris, as we see mobile phones and other digital techniques leapfrogging old technologies to reach the global poor.[36]

CHRIS: Well, to be honest, my initial response would be more of a 'yes, but'. I thought we were going to get to the nitty-gritty of planet saving. Is that really your solution, some new digital gimmick or technology?

MIKE: Well, if we ever do crack the problem of fusion energy...but, no...I agree...this is stuff to keep our eye on and definitely worth including in the discussion, but none of it looks quick enough or definite enough to be much more than my self-indulgent side issue for now. But I would say it's what you should pray for, since it's one hell of a lot easier to imagine this sort of technological fix working than the alternative, to which I now turn.

I think our last meeting had quite an impact upon me. I clearly was guilty of mixing up moral and practical issues, where saving the planet was really a route to various utopian ideas about putting us back in touch with nature, living in harmony and all legitimated by the necessity of sustainability. But I would now acknowledge the force of Grace's argument about decoupling measures directly relating to climate change from saving our souls and ascetic anti-materialism. So, if I strip away all that other stuff, I guess what I come down to, my bedrock as it were in the sense of consistency, is one that reflects what I do, day by day, as a professional academic. I grew up with the critique of positivism, the epistemological idea that we can only trust what we observe,[37] and have lived through several versions of the attempts to contextualise science as a social practice, whose latest avatar is perhaps the work of Bruno Latour.[38] As a social scientist, I am sceptical about absolute truths and claims to proof.

CHRIS: I can already see a 'but'...

MIKE: Yes, indeed. But...actually, I think, if you really want to make a serious critique of the likes of economics or psychology...

GRACE: Don't forget evolutionary anthropologists. They are the heretics I really can't stand.

MIKE: OK, whoever, whatever. My point is that it is far better to make this critique from a position which is essentially one of fully embracing the natural sciences. I tend to shock my students in my respect for natural science as an approach to the physical world. I don't think I am naïve. I assume scientists, just as much as social scientists, pick their best results, the ones they want to see, and manage to evade the ones that don't make them look as good. I know science as practice is cultural. But I also know I would be a hypocrite not to acknowledge how much I rely on technologies that started as science. When you work on climate change, which is one of the most aggregate and inexact fields, you also see how scientists still retain a scholarly approach to probabilities. In fact, the more data they have collected, the wider have become the predicted temperature changes.[39] They are quite sensitive to different interpretations and certainly to the insecurities of prediction. But in the end they know they are responsible for making the case that comes closest to the evidence from a thousand scientists working on a thousand different sources of data, and they do the best job they can with those statistics. I understand Miller's problem with epistemology, but I take him to be arguing that the core problem is not natural science but the inappropriate application of these procedures to an economy that is largely cultural. And I agree with Grace in her opposition to evolutionary studies, that this goes for most of human behaviour also, which is why I share her scepticism of experimental psychology. But the reason people find the economists and psychologists plausible is because they have learnt to sound like natural scientists, and every day we see the successes of natural science and how it gets us our food, energy and many other systems.

CHRIS: No, no, no, no, no! Sorry, but this is all too glib and simplistic. I don't yet know where you are going with this, but you still have this simple image of chemicals reacting in a lab that are predictable and replicable. But, as you just said, climate is the aggregate of vast numbers of different forces, often fortuitously juxtaposed, which does make it more like social science.[40] And your current stance seems to be ignoring pretty much every single argument that you yourself put forward through your reading of Hulme's *Why We Disagree on Climate Change*. His book wasn't just some bland statement that culture makes a difference. Every chapter showed how and why and what difference culture makes. Look, I am not some diehard post-modern relativist. If we are going to quote from life then, sure, the fact the three of us mark an essay on, say, politics and expect to come up with a similar grade means we have shared canons of evidence and scholarship. But that's partly because of shared expectations and ideology. Anyway, to be frank, this sounds like academic throat clearing. How does flying the flag for natural science lead to practical solutions?

MIKE: OK, I expected this would be touching raw nerves. Science and epistemology are where you find the basic compatibilities and incompatibilities of academics. But, in a way, it may not matter too much where exactly a person sits on the line between my sense of science and Chris's. Remember the line we used on that anti-cuts demonstration: 'If you think knowledge is expensive, then try ignorance.' My point is that, however complex, cultural, interpretive and problematic science is held to be, it is because of scientific evidence that I accept climate change, and, yes, my own ship sails closer to George Monbiot than to Hulme.

But the reason this matters? It's just that I would argue that, if our understanding of the problem comes from science, then that should also be our route to the solution. Not from pseudo-sciences like economics but from natural science. Sure, there are a vast number of influences here all tangled up together, but we have to take responsibility for working out the priorities. What I really want to know right now, at this point in time, as precisely as possible, is which are the chemicals, which are the processes, which are the practices that contribute most to these problems of climate change and in which way? Of the thousand things that pollute, which are the most urgent and most culpable? Is it black soot, or some obscure minor ingredient in aerosol cans I have never heard of? What is the aggregate effect of air conditioning as against central heating, or this pesticide as against that one? To start talking about taking practical action surely means getting deeply involved in the nitty-gritty of what actions exactly will make what kind of real impact.

I know that at one level it's that geeky side of me that adores those little question and answer sessions in the newspaper, that wants to know whether the energy used in a hot-air dryer in a toilet is more or less than that used in making and disposing the alternative of paper towels.[41] I have that childish belief that knowing the science will tell me what to think. But is it just childish, or is it actually what we really need to know to make decisions? I want to know which things create short-term damage, which last in the atmosphere ten thousand years, which block sunlight, and which are problematic because they are running out. In a world where electronics depend on rare earths, and where biofuels seem to be a good idea when grown in Brazil but terrible when grown in Germany, I want to see the world systematically audited for environmental consequences. I don't want proofs, but I would rather have evidence-based estimates than pig ignorance. I am actually quite a sceptic over the more ideological stances on topics such as GM foods, which may well have a positive impact on poverty. Rather, I am looking for clear evidence that a certain product interacts with the atmosphere to create global warming, or the effects of a given toxin on the food chain can be linked with pollution and disease, and the levels we can still employ that will not have such an impact.

I agree with Grace about not leaving this to public perception. If we did that, we would inevitably concentrate on those things the public can see in front of their noses and that make them feel better, since they refer to actions they themselves can take, such as replacing disposable supermarket bags with recycling. But as Berners-Lee comments, 'For your carrier bags to have the same footprint as one trip to Hong Kong you would have to go to the supermarket every single day for 10 years and return each time with 93 disposable bags.'[42] He is talking about a regular flight. Business class takes more room and more carbon miles. So, once armed with that knowledge, you switch priorities. You appreciate that what would really make a difference in my digital sustainability programme is encouraging webcam and virtual conference facilities, which can make nine out of ten business trips by air unnecessary.[43]

GRACE: As though people go to conferences and meetings actually to conduct work...

MIKE: You can scoff, but you know sometimes they do, and would be happy not to have to leave their families if they could work with video conferencing instead. But, seriously, right now we need the courage to make priorities that don't accord with public assumptions and preferences. Again, public opinion and popular academia see globalisation and global trade as a key problem, but science says the opposite. The vast majority of international trade goes by shipping, which is relatively low in energy use, while trying to make each country self-sufficient in its own production would be vastly more wasteful of our resources.[44] I know you dislike quantification, but that's because it is so misapplied that scientific significance becomes reduced to misleading statistical significance. But good analysis is the best guide to understanding what actually is going on, and I really want to understand these things better.

GRACE: OK, so you read and read and read, and you get yourself as informed as you can, and then? So now you can win all the arguments at climate change conventions, so what?

MIKE: Sorry, I was over-personalising, over-indulging if you like. It is the collective knowledge we require, not that I personally have to know these things. We need those intergovernmental panels on climate change to expand into intergovernmental panels on the precise consequences of particular acts of consumption. Because it seems to me that the solutions have to come from regulation, but regulation that goes way back to the sources of consumption itself – in other words, to production. Whatever consumption is about, it is inextricably linked to production. When I was travelling around China, the visible sign of planetary destruction came from factories and smog. You told me at our last meeting about that book on the environmental impacts of the global aluminium industry that, to be honest, I hadn't known about. So I went away and read it, and, yes, it is entirely horrific. And it made one of my key points very well, that the reason we don't spend so much time these days pointing the finger at production is simply because we have exported extraction industries to the developing world. We only get worried when it's on our doorstep, like that toxic sludge issue from bauxite extraction in Hungary, and even more when it's a BP spill around New Orleans, but most of the production issues have become sort of 'out of sight, out of mind'.

So, for me, it is all about prioritising which goods and which chemicals and which processes are most problematic and then stopping them at source. If you don't want to go to consumer choice, and you don't want to go to markets for your solutions, then you have to go to international regulation, based not on the authorities of consumers or voters, but on that professional authority that comes within science. I want to cede authority upwards rather than downwards, although I know that is deeply unfashionable in an increasingly liberal world. So what I am saying is we need international science bodies that literally lay down the law as to what substances need to be banned, what processes curtailed, largely at the level of production, rather than worrying about consumers and their choices.

Many of the things that need to be done can be done at this level. The problem of cars is exemplified by gas guzzlers with large engines. But why should car engines over a certain size even exist? There are limits you can put on food miles. Why not have a complete ban on the importation of bottled still water to countries where tap water is known to be safe? Think of the huge amount of energy wasted in office blocks with their air conditioning turned down so low that you come in from tropical heat and have to pile on clothes because you are freezing. So such units should be set so they can't go below a level of generally consensual comfort – say, 23 degrees – and companies are fined if they try and overrule the mechanism. This means consulting not just with natural scientists. There is a whole flurry of good new social science on the issue of cultural norms and comfort when it comes to things like the temperature of rooms.[45] Behind such evident consumption lie all the regulations that pertain to manufacturing, which plastic should and should not be made, what agricultural feed should not be made from, and what industrial processes cause unacceptable emissions. If we agree that choice is not the solution, then we have to bite the bullet and say regulation is.

GRACE: Well, it seems we still have the capacity to surprise each other. Because my impression was that the greens tend to go in the opposite direction. Most greens may not like free markets, but they tend to be liberals in politics and lean to decentralisation rather than trusting anonymous and secretive world bodies dictating to us what we should and shouldn't do.[46] But, more generally, as a result of Kyoto and Copenhagen, there seems to be a growing consensus about the sheer utopianism of ideals of global or international agreements that could ever create such regulations. It's surely pretty clear by now that the US government isn't about to concede much in this direction even if the rest of the world were to come to agreement about banning this or curbing that, which also looks less rather than more likely. Most actual stuff happens at the national level. We may have problems with markets, and we may have been brought up with socialist ideals about states – Chris, bless him, is still living those dreams – but it simply doesn't happen.[47] So what's the point in coming up with solutions at a level of the deeply improbable and unfeasible?

MIKE: Of course, I'm well aware of these texts about the environment and politics. I teach three lectures on the topic. But, in a way, that's my point. The evidence from those books is that the politics we looked to for solutions has become instead the brick wall we hit our heads against. If what I just described is read as a political project, then it is doomed to the quicksands of international 'dialogue'. As Pielke[48] has recently shown, if there is one reason that the efforts towards alleviating climate change have gone into reverse, it is precisely the over-politicisation of the issues. But beneath the radar of politics there is a vast subterranean world of global and national regulation that is operating quite successfully because it is largely depoliticised. Global technologies, including the internet, work through global regulations, providing standards for the stuff that really counts, such as aircraft maintenance and air traffic control more generally. There are plenty of global bans of all sorts of toxic and problematic substances. Look at the procedures of medical approval – there is a vast arena of regulation that works mainly because it is seen as back-office stuff. We, the public, don't pretend to understand it, so we don't much care about it. We are much more concerned that things just work. There is more and more regulation each year that we just take for granted, unless it goes wrong.

This has to be linked to the point I just made about moving the focus from consumption to production.

Consumption is the arena of public awareness and, therefore, inevitably a politicised world where agreements can't and won't happen. But most people haven't the vaguest clue as to what regulations apply in factories, because they don't see them and they don't really care about them. So that is where the regulations should apply. If we want to ban the use of a chemical, we can check its presence much more easily at the moment of production than in subsequent dispersed consumption. There are far fewer factories than homes. Most of the work that has to be done to create less energy inefficiency in terms of consumption of goods can best be achieved through the transformation in the processing of the materials – by regulation in steel manufacture or the selection and creation of plastics.

Have you ever heard of the European Commission on Mobility and Transport or the Federal Aviation Administration? No, you just fly. Yet think for a minute about the vast amount of regulation that must exist behind aviation. All of us experience cars breaking down from time to time, but if an aircraft in flight broke down we would experience that just the once. The safety record of mass aviation is nothing short of miraculous. There are vast arenas of regulation we just take for granted that pertain to almost every area of life, from plastics to medicines. When the internet developed, it of necessity spawned instruments such as ICANN[49] for specialist issues like domain names and work with broader intellectual property regimes, such as WIPO[50] and more generally the WTO. That is the level at which regulations have to emerge.

Because actually we don't live in a liberal world. We live in a world which seems open and free at the highly superficial level, of that which we actually see and are aware of and can be bothered to be concerned about. But, beneath that, our security and welfare depend on an intensely regulated and policed world of standards and safeguards and restrictions. We focus on these only when they fail, and then we protest bitterly that someone died, as we then put it, 'needlessly'. I want the planet saved through arcane regulations about things most of us don't understand, but which can determine what will and will not be made. Even if we know that science isn't at all apolitical, most people believe that it is, and curiously that's a considerable advantage right now, because it means people will accept its strictures to the degree this remains apparently depoliticised. So, if Grace is right and the planet isn't going to be saved by moral agendas, and Chris is right that it won't be saved by political agendas, then surely it has to be saved by technical agendas?

CHRIS: Mike, one thing that comes over as quite charming, if that doesn't sound too condescending, is you clearly know your faults. If you keep quoting aviation I suspect it's partly because you are way off having your feet on the ground. It's the same geek tendencies that dream technological fixes and that keep you so divorced from the social aspects of our problem. It is just fine for a bunch of scientists to pontificate about what they think we need to do to prevent climate change, but that wouldn't even start to address the point that Grace and I made at the start of our discussion about modern China. A solution is not something you propose; it is something people actually accept. These regulatory authorities are not wise elders sitting in Platonic caves determining our welfare from on high. Once they come to the practical level of enforcement, they are riddled with horse-trading national politics.

Funnily enough, I think sometimes that being a socialist means I actually pay more attention and have more respect than some others for the sheer ability of business to get things done. Actually, if we ask what so far has been achieved by way of green goals, much of it is at the local level, the initiatives of local communities and councils. But equally in the vanguard are often major industries. It is the companies themselves who are most innovative at trying to become carbon neutral, who actually understand that this is in their long-term interest. In fact, in some cases, such as insurance companies that pay out on natural disasters, it's pretty obviously in their short-term interests too.[51]

I would not dispute your starting point. Surely we do need to be discussing regulation, and much of it is technical. I am the one who tends to defend faceless bureaucrats whom everyone else despises because I respect their fundamental contribution to the project of equality. But the key is how to make this thing work. Because, while I agree that the issue is not one of consumer choice, I do think it is always going to be one of consumer acquiescence. These regulations may be essential, but they are going to create prohibitions on things that people actually want, and societies have long histories of getting around such prohibitions unless they in some sense or other support them. Surely the internet is at least as much a story of how we can ignore regulations and get around them as of how we can create them.

What I was trying to say when we met last time was that you are never going to be able to divorce consumption issues from the wider context of social issues such as inequality. Remember *The Spirit Level* and the desire for advancement among peoples all around the world who feel like second-class citizens simply because they have less. I know you both think I am a one-trick pony, that I try and push everything back to social inequality. But, oddly enough, I think you have reached the point where that is the single determinant factor that will make or break your solutions. Indeed, once you start to think about those social aspects, you are led in exactly the opposite direction from your trajectory. The point is not for people to see less, but for them to see more.

There is one reason above all why a market solution to climate change is just flying pigs. And it is because markets will simply exacerbate the issues of inequality that drive so much of consumption and desire. And we have agreed this is a question not of greed, but of sheer unfairness. People in developing countries are not going to agree to curb consumption until they achieve the levels of developed countries. Surely that was the single most important lesson from Copenhagen and its ancillary meetings. And it has been Grace's main argument from the very start. We can't solve one intractable issue of climate change outside of an even more intractable issue of equality. This may sound like resigned defeatism, but actually I think it provides a better route to practical solutions than yours, Mike.

MIKE: Practical solution? Listen, it was your lot that caused our problems. By the time benign-sounding socialism reached the level of Pol Pot, any credibility for a socialist agenda was shot, and we end up with generations where even my students think that the smartest kind of radical is some anti-state anarchism and that freedom is something achieved by pure individuals outside of law, which makes them seem to me just as liberal as the neo-liberal economies they are deluded into thinking they are fighting. They simply can't see that it is law that protects freedom for individuals and state regulations that are the only curb on corporations.

CHRIS: What do you mean, 'your lot'? I wasn't actually marching on behalf of Pol Pot. You seem to have forgotten my socialism is actually not very far from our mutually beloved Norwegian social democracy; it's about protecting the welfare state, not enforcing tyranny.

MIKE: All right, I got carried away. But I still think you are reducing our agreed priority of today to your past priorities.

CHRIS: Well then, let me fill in the details. One of my PhD students, Gabrielle Hosein, carried out her research in Trinidad on politics with a small p – the micro-politics of local markets and local political patronage.[52] It was revelatory in helping us understand how the principle of perceived fairness impinges right across the whole political spectrum. It wasn't that people were for or against the state, it was whether they felt the state's authority equated with their sense of reasonable enforcement of reasonable positions. Even within Chinese repression people seem to come out against the unfairness of corrupt officialdom. I mentioned last time it's defence at the grandest scale in Amartya Sen's recent book on justice,[53] but equally Will Hutton has just produced four hundred pages not just about how fairness got booted out of British politics, but both the necessity and, even more importantly, the means by which it can be brought back in.[54]

Now, why does fairness matter at this juncture? The critical point is that Mike can have all the science he likes, all the regulatory consensus, and adjudication as to what needs to be done and what to prioritise, but people have to accept those rulings, and this depends upon how that is done. Saving a planet can't be like some guilty secret. My argument is simply that people will accept curbs on consumption to the degree, and only to the degree, that these are transparently fair. If some people continue to get away with still having the things that they have been forbidden, then ultimately these restrictions will fail and become part of an entirely different struggle over power and authority.

So let us say that Mike's scientists agree that no car engine size should be over 1.6 litres, or that no freezer can be made with a certain liquid, or that all new builds will have to include the cost of a particular kind of insulation, or that a chemical used in cotton cleaning or as a pesticide is banned. If they determine that something is destructive to the planet then, yes, I agree with Mike that we simply shouldn't allow it to be produced in the first place. But, unlike Mike, I am directing attention to the potential consumers. If an engine of 1.6 litres is the limit, then it doesn't matter if you are a billionaire or living in the US or wherever, such engines cannot be made and should be confiscated where found. No persons and no places should be privileged. If the cheaper but dangerous process is banned, then it must not be hidden; it must be seen to be banned – evidently, everywhere and equally.

I really do believe that, if people see that new regulations are being enforced on the principle of fairness, that the richest cannot escape them either – neither the richest countries nor the richest individuals – then I can see far more chance of consumer acquiescence in these new regimes and limitations. The concept of fair regulation only works in a state of complete simplicity, one with no exceptions, no compromise. Transparency is the key. Absolute bans are much easier to enforce than compromised bans that come with exceptions and equivocations. You may not agree with all my *Spirit Level* argument for the righteousness of equality in itself, just as you don't have to agree with Grace's arguments about the consequences of consumption. Those are arguments we can continue to drink over and debate about as long as our livers and lives permit. So, yes, take the best consensus you can from those with the best authority you can and turn these into simple clear regulations without exceptions. I think Miller was right in rejecting earlier theories that see consumption as driven largely by competitive emulation. But what I think still counts is this basic sense of fairness which is offended when you see that others have what you don't have for no good reason other than birth or corruption. So let's use that absolute character of the ban based on science and apply it absolutely, without fear or favour, and then I think you may get acceptance.

GRACE: I am really getting more than a little confused, because you seem to be agreeing with Mike under the guise of disagreeing. In which case, why doesn't your solution suffer from the same problems of utopian internationalism – regulations that sound good but won't ever happen? How do you get the US Tea Party to agree to impose universal regulations and curbs based on the ideal of equality? How do you get people whose mascot is the Hummer to agree to have no engine sizes bigger than 1.6 litres? The green agenda needs to learn from the failures of the red, otherwise it just repeats the mistakes, of which the most important was its authoritarianism. Greens think they are not just right but that they embody the authority of moral necessity: they simply *have* to save the planet, so pretty much anything is justified. But so did socialism, which is why it so often ended up resorting to violence. Actually, I see two males agreeing on highly authoritarian solutions – surprise, surprise. We may convince ourselves that we need to save the planet by this or that regulation, but we don't have the authority simply to impose this on the world. For all its faults, I will always go for due democratic process. My own country has suffered long enough from the paternalistic arrogance of benign and less benign oligarchy.

CHRIS: Excuse me, but you have this back to front. My point was to show how you can get consensus by paying attention to fairness. It was Mike who thought he can impose science regardless by the back door. Sure, the US Tea Party wouldn't accept such restrictions. More problematically, I am not at all sure that US Democrats would either. But, actually, if you look at the lessons of recent debates, the US is more the exception than the rule. Much of the rest of the world is part of a gradual but insistent movement towards the acknowledgment of these issues. The Europeans represent a huge block, and the main issues between them and the BRIC countries[55] are precisely those of fairness. If you have Europe and BRIC on board, which for the kinds of issues we have just been discussing I think is feasible, then you have most of the world. You don't need the US to ratify in the first instance. If we say no cars at all will be acceptable with an engine larger than 1.6 litres, or set so they can't go above a certain speed, then you can't import cars from the US. And US manufacturers depend on global markets for their profitability. The only really major international change we need is a transformation in the rules and attitude of the WTO to differentiate genuine environmental concerns from old-fashioned protectionism, which – I agree with Mike here – doesn't do much for climate change concerns either.

As it happens, outside of these trade networks the world is much less of a global place than we have come to believe.[56] You don't need to start from vast and unwieldy international consensus; you can build up from the kind of national-based political and regulatory will that we can already see is feasible. By the way, I didn't deign to discuss the suggestion that regulation is somehow male. I mean, come on, Grace, you don't really want to leave a denuded planet to our children because regulation isn't feminine?

GRACE: That's not what...

MIKE (oblivious to the last exchange):   OK, I have been digesting this. Certainly I have no problem at all with a focus upon equality and fairness in the delivery, but the starting point needs to be to get natural science out of the grip of economic pseudo-science and give it the autonomy to determine our priorities. Then we need rapidly to implement regulations, but equally innovations that create genuine reductions in harmful emissions. When it comes to your issue of acquiescence, the problem is that the generation I teach watched cartoons like *Captain Planet*, in which the superheroes were green but the villains were always scientists in white lab coats. Yet it is these two groups who most need to work together.

GRACE: OK, so then let's work on this problem of acquiescence. Because, just as Mike's arguments about scientific authority sound naïve to Chris – that is, consensus in science is not much use without addressing the politics of its implementation – so my dear husband's political consensus around fairness in implementation still sounds naïve to me. I don't think politics is ever going to recapture that degree of authority. But you are right that, unless people are willing to accept them, prohibitions rarely work. They might in terms of airline regulation, since there isn't a constituency out there who have any great desire for airlines to fail. But if you ban cars with engines larger than 1.6 litres, then there are going to be all sorts of people who suddenly think life is not worth living unless they get 1.8 litres, and if there is public sympathy then there will be ways around such regulations.

MIKE: That's it. Grace you have done it – inadvertently, but you have done it.

GRACE: Sorry, done what exactly?

MIKE: Done what you promised to do from the start: worked out the context in which my educational scheme makes sense and has a major role to play.

GRACE: Really?

MIKE: Sure, think about it. What we are now saying is this. We do have a potential plan – more importantly, I think a plausible plan – to address climate change. Not simple, not straightforward, but plausible, which is what we promised ourselves. I think ultimately it was essential to have that background that we gained through reading Miller. Because that put a spoke in the wheel of what I admit had been my own rather naïve and general anti-consumerism. Combined with Grace's point about saving the planet being more than a lifestyle choice, it convinced me that I have been going about this quite the wrong way. Simple anti-consumerism is actually making things worse, because it confuses and conflates different issues. So my earlier point is that, instead, we have to isolate precisely those practices and substances that are most problematic for the future of our planet and put the focus squarely on them. I think when it comes to issues of production and industry then I will stick to my earlier argument that this requires simply the kind of background regulatory authority that already exists for countless problematic materials, from medicines to pollutants, and we just need to get on with the job of linking good science to effective regulation. Ideally this should work beneath the radar of overt politics. But I also think that Chris is half right because, when it comes to changes in consumer goods, maybe these will only work when everything is transparent and fair. But I think this too is feasible, providing we deal with Grace's final objection, which is the question of how we retain the acquiescence of populations. But that's exactly where my educational scheme comes in. I think the reason you didn't follow it up before was that you assumed my plan was to persuade kids to turn to green consumption once they were directly confronted by the evidence for the consequences of their consumption. And, yes, maybe it was and, yes again, maybe you are right that this would have been naïve. But if, instead, we say that the aim of my scheme is not to get people to choose green of their own volition, but rather simply to acquiesce in political changes that are required for the protection of the planet, then I really do think what could work is something that puts consumption and its consequences into the heart of education by teaching on the basis of products that the children actually consume themselves. In fact, it would be essential. I really do think it would build the kind of consciousness of these issues so that at least we would not collectively object to the required regulations and would support the authority required to enforce them. If that is the case, then finally we have the long- and the short-term measures in place, where the long term is directed towards our children – and that works for your point too, Chris, since if there is one group that is single-mindedly focused upon fairness it's surely the kids.

GRACE: Which reminds me that actually we really need to leave now and pick up our own kids. But in any case that was a pretty rousing conclusion, Mike, and, yes, on that basis I think I can warm to your educational scheme, which I admit sounded a bit hare-brained when you first described it, but now seems like the cornerstone to the edifice we have constructed.

CHRIS: Grace is right: we really do have to go now. But let me conform to type with the final word, which is actually just to thank you, Mike, both for the original idea and seeing it through and for your generous hospitality today. We agreed that our next meeting would be to compare our courses and reading lists on consumption, and that we would meet at the Bree Louise pub near Euston, which has a great beer selection, and I have a CAMRA[57] card to the ready.

MIKE: With hopefully also some return to these matters, because I would like to add some extra flesh to a set of promising bones.

GRACE: Agreed.

Postscript

At this point I need to give my thanks to Chris, Grace and Mike for their respective contributions, but also to usher them back behind the curtain and come forward and take the flack as the author of this book. My main claim to any authority for its contents would derive from many years of carrying out ethnographic studies of consumption. Where this book strays more into the consequences of consumption, such as the wider political economy or climate change, I have relied far more on other academics and their arguments. But clearly I felt that to write a book about consumption should include taking responsibility for at least commenting upon these consequences, which could hardly be more consequential.

If you review the logic of the book as a whole, there is a central argument that most discussions around the consequences of consumption stem from a mistaken understanding of consumption itself as a process. If these discussions are to progress, then the misapprehensions need to be corrected. What usually happens is that critical academics with important points to make of a red or green variety project onto consumption that which they would wish or need it to be in order to make their arguments. Left-wing critics claim consumption is largely fostered by advertising and demand is created by commerce. These goods then contribute to practices of status emulation, which in turn can be related back to capitalism's other consequence in fostering of class and social inequality. The left holds on to these beliefs because, if this is true, they provide a relatively straightforward target. Get rid of these causes – for example, abolish advertising or reduce class differences – and demand will collapse. Furthermore, all these reductions in consumption would in any case be beneficial to society. Unfortunately it is plausible to imagine a Norway that banned advertising, reduced social inequality still further, and constricted business until it was closer to socialism than capitalism. My prediction is that demand for goods would remain largely unchanged, because the things that consumption is being used for in chapters 2, 3 and 4 would remain entirely unchanged. Greens embrace a still wider perspective and generally a still more convenient one, which associates consumption in general with materialism, thus giving them a moral high ground to condemn consumption and equate saving the planet with saving our souls. I don't accept their premise, which is clearly contradicted by my evidence. What I do support is both these green and red aspirations regarding the imperative to increase and protect the welfare both of populations and of the planet. I share some, but only some, of their wider moral ideals. My own particular focus would be resolutely on the moral imperative to end poverty and deprivation, which is something I am constantly confronted with in carrying out fieldwork in various parts of the world. I see poverty as absolutely debilitating and grossly unfair.

So an argument that we have misunderstood consumption and its causes is far more important than merely a question of an academic corrective, a concern with some version of truth and education, though this alone would be a sufficient motive to be fully engaged with such debates. The core three chapters in this book provide evidence for an alternative view on what consumption is. The chapters on ethnographic studies of Trinidad as a consumer society, shopping in London and why we buy blue jeans are intended to convince you that consumption is mainly about quite different things. Status emulation and materialism may exist, but they are of minor relevance compared to the incorporation of this vast array of material difference in the expression of complex social relationships and wider cosmologies. Many of these, such as love and the struggle to be ordinary, would be seen as largely positive and equate with that richness of diversity we call culture. A whole prior book, *Stuff*, was written to show just how such material things act as culture, and that book adds substantially more evidence to support the central point of these three chapters.

But my point in *Stuff* was not to adjudicate goods as good or bad. The term 'material culture' is intended to be neutral. The ethnography merely shows that goods are utilised within an extraordinary and expressive field of cultural life, where we use them to help delineate our values, cosmology, emotional repertoires, and sense of sameness and difference, and, as with other cultural forms, for entertainment, communication and adding to our capacities within everyday life.

Capitalism is certainly the context for this engagement, but I have argued that it is as much consequence as cause. Other societies that do not or did not have capitalism, ranging from ancient Rome or medieval Japan to recent attempts at socialism, were just as readily engaged with consumption and material culture. It is a travesty of anthropology to think that people with fewer goods, such as Australian Aboriginal society or Amazonian tribes, were more functionalist or more concerned with what they needed. Pretty much the entirety of my discipline of anthropology says the opposite. What little they have is used, above all, for wondrously creative acts of cosmology. They impress because they are typically so adept at turning nature into fantastic cultural constellations. If in doubt, read some anthropology of Amazonia or Melanesia.

My point is that we will get nowhere if we start by being dismissive of consumption itself, or by thinking that we could somehow remove its causes. Social relations are the primary cause of consumption. This is the message that apparently no one wants to hear because it is supremely inconvenient to the moral and other goals we have set ourselves. Instead, let us accept that consumption is central to our contemporary life and tease out its nuances from the public use of state systems to clothing wardrobes, from housing to new digital lives. But we can't then just leave commerce as a black box. We also need to engage critically with studies of business and realise that, if we apply the same ethnographic methods to finance and retail, we can break through their ideologies and representations and see how, in practice, this is also a complex of everyday infrastructures that need to be understood in their own right and not allow academics to obfuscate by replacing them with images of idealised or demonised economic models. I am much more inclined to the critique of capitalisms than of consumption because, except where it is curbed, as within social-democratic politics, there is plenty of evidence that, in its many forms, capitalism comes to serve its own interests rather than those of welfare, with evident results such as vast gulfs in inequality that, contrary to its claims, are completely unrelated to its potential for supplying us with goods. To this critique we need to add the urgency of confronting the issue of climate change. A transformation in our understanding of consumption means that we turn from grand and simplistic critiques of consumption per se. Instead we take climate change seriously as its own agenda. We use our science and scholarship to separate out clearly those changes which evidence shows are necessary for planet-saving purposes. Getting rid of these pernicious substances and practices will be a whole lot easier if we no longer think we have to curb consumption as a whole or deny the contribution of both commerce and consumer goods to the elimination of poverty and the advancement of welfare.

It is probable that many readers were disappointed that, between them, Chris, Mike and Grace did not come up with some simpler and more easily administered panaceas for quickly dealing with climate change. I am afraid they could no more than reflect my own limited understanding and imagination. I have no rabbits in my hats – actually I don't even have hats. But I still feel that their contributions were radical with respect to current trajectories. Through them I have sought to show that the main solutions being advocated at present are not just wrong but profoundly mistaken. I really do believe that putting economic theory, which more than any other factor has been responsible for creating this mess, in charge of finding a solution is the primary reason why we are failing. New markets and more consumer choice are not going to stop climate change. Instead, I have advocated a series of shorter- and longer-term measures. The science of climate change could lead much more directly to regulation, often at the point of production, that bans the most problematic culprits. Where these seep into the area of consumption, then transparency and, above all, fairness is key to their acceptance, as are these longer-term changes that make awareness of cause and effect central to our education system. My aim is not simply to provoke yet more debates between interested academics. I have tried to write in an accessible manner because I think the issues raised in this book matter today more than ever, and what I really want is for the results of our academic research also to be consumed with consequences.

Notes

Prologue

1 At the time of writing *Stuff*, my working title for this second volume was *Consumed by Doubt*, which has been replaced by this new title.

Chapter 1 What's Wrong with Consumption?

1 D. Meadows et al., *The Limits to Growth: A Report for the Club of Rome's Project on the Predicament of Mankind* (New York: New American Library, 1972).
2 L. Grant, *We Had it So Good* (London: Virago, 2011).
3 Intergovernmental Panel on Climate Change, *Fourth Assessment Report: Climate Change 2007*, 3 vols (Cambridge: Cambridge University Press, 2007); N. Stern, *The Economics of Climate Change* (Cambridge: Cambridge University Press, 2006).
4 M. Hulme, *Why We Disagree about Climate Change* (Cambridge: Cambridge University Press, 2009); G. Monbiot, *Heat: How to Stop the Planet Burning* (London: Allen Lane, 2006).
5 B. Latour, *We Have Never Been Modern* (Hemel Hempstead: Harvester Wheatsheaf, 1993).
6 R. Layard, *Happiness: Lessons for a New Science* (2nd edn, London: Penguin, 2011).
7 R. Easterlin, 'Does economic growth improve the human lot?', in P. David and M. Reder, eds, *Nations and Households in Economic*

Growth: Essays in Honor of Moses Abramovitz (New York: Academic Press, 1974).

8 For a summary, see A. Oswald, 'The well-being of nations', *Times Higher Education*, 19 May 2011, pp. 35–9.

9 For my own research on Filipino migration, see M. Madianou and D. Miller, *Migration and New Media: Transnational Families and Polymedia* (London: Routledge, 2012).

10 E. Shove, *Comfort, Cleanliness and Convenience* (Oxford: Berg, 2003).

11 A. Clarke, 'As seen on TV: design and domestic economy', in M. Andrews and M. Talbot, eds, *All the World and her Husband: Women in Twentieth-Century Consumer Culture* (London: Cassell, 2000), pp. 146–61.

12 H. Hubert and M. Mauss, *Sacrifice: Its Nature and Functions* (Chicago: University of Chicago Press, 1964); see also D. Miller, *A Theory of Shopping* (Cambridge: Polity, 1998), pp. 73–110.

13 K. Humphrey, *Excess: Anti-Consumerism in the West* (Cambridge: Polity, 2010).

14 For example, J. de Graaf, D. Wann and T. Naylor, *Affluenza: The All-Consuming Epidemic* (San Francisco: Berrett-Koehler, 2001).

15 Typical of this ilk would be Z. Bauman, *Consuming Life* (Cambridge: Polity, 2007), and J. Schor, *The Overspent American* (New York: Harper Perennial, 1999).

16 For example, K. Soper and F. Trentmann, eds, *Citizenship and Consumption* (London: Palgrave, 2008).

17 U. Sonesson, B. Mattsson, T. Nybrant and T. Ohlsson, 'Industrial processing versus home cooking: an environmental comparison between three ways to prepare a meal', *Ambio*, 34/4–5 (2005): 414–42, cited in R. Wilk, 'Consuming ourselves to death', in S. Crate and M. Nuttall, eds, *Anthropology and Climate Change* (Walnut Creek, CA: Left Coast Press, 2009), pp. 265–76.

18 J. Davidson, *Courtesans and Fishcakes* (London: Fontana, 1998).

19 T. Veblen, *The Theory of the Leisure Class: An Economic Study of Institutions* (New York: Mentor, 1899).

20 For an excellent review of the centrality of morality to US writing on consumption, see the two-volume history by D. Horowitz, *The Morality of Spending: Attitudes Toward the Consumer Society in America, 1875–1940* (Chicago: Ivan R. Dee, 1992), and *The Anxieties of Affluence: Critiques of American Consumer Culture, 1939–1979* (Amherst: University of Massachusetts Press, 2005).

21 M. Douglas and B. Isherwood, *The World of Goods* (London: Allen Lane, 1979).

22 M. Douglas and M. Nicod, 'Taking the biscuit', *New Society*, 19 December 1974, pp. 774–7.
23 P. Bourdieu, *Distinction: A Social Critique of the Judgement of Taste* (London: Routledge & Kegan Paul, 1984).
24 Probably the best current introduction to the study of consumption in social science is R. Sassatelli, *Consumer Culture: History, Theory and Politics* (London: Sage, 2007).
25 R. Wilkinson and K. Pickett, *The Spirit Level: Why More Equal Societies Almost Always Do Better* (London: Penguin, 2010).
26 For similar sentiments, see D. McCloskey, *Bourgeois Dignity: Why Economics Can't Explain the Modern World* (Chicago: University of Chicago Press, 2010), pp. 60–5.
27 Ibid., p. 13.
28 Ibid., p. 218.
29 At the Hay and Wye festival – 'Howthelightgetsin', June 2011.
30 A. Sen, *The Idea of Justice* (London: Allen Lane, 2009).
31 F. Padel and S. Das, *Out of This Earth: East India Adivasis and the Aluminium Cartel* (New Delhi: Orient Black Swan, 2010).
32 BBC Radio, 4 June 2011.
33 Compare P. Hanson, *Advertising and Socialism* (New York: International Arts and Sciences Press, 1974), with S. Drakulić, *How We Survived Communism and Even Laughed* (New York: Harper Perennial, 1992).

Chapter 2   A Consumer Society

1 The term 'culture' is used frequently in this volume. I use the word as synonymous with the concept of objectification. The theory behind this is given in D. Miller, *Material Culture and Mass Consumption* (Oxford: Blackwell, 1987) and summarised in D. Miller, *Stuff* (Cambridge: Polity, 2010), pp. 54–68).
2 The country consists of two islands, Trinidad and Tobago, but Tobago has a very different history and population, and my writing is therefore restricted to the island of Trinidad.
3 V.S. Naipaul, *The Mimic Men* (London: André Deutsch, 1967).
4 See 'Coca-Cola: a black sweet drink from Trinidad', in D. Miller, ed., *Material Cultures* (Chicago: University of Chicago Press, 1998), pp. 169–88. For the work of other anthropologists on the local meaning of these drinks, see R. Foster, *Coca-Globalization: Following Soft Drinks from New York to New Guinea* (New York: Palgrave Macmillan, 2008); D. Gewertz and F. Errington, 'On PepsiCo

and piety in a Papua New Guinea "modernity"', *American Ethnologist*, 23/3 (1996): 476–93.

5 For a useful history, see M. Pendergrast, *For God, Country and Coca-Cola* (London: Weidenfeld & Nicolson, 1993).

6 In writing this I am acutely aware that there exists a whole field of evolutionary anthropology which tends to take such analogies literally. I don't. The study of evolution will teach you absolutely zilch about human beings and consumption; it's just a metaphor.

7 Much of the content of this chapter comes from D. Miller, *Modernity: An Ethnographic Approach* (Oxford: Berg, 1994); and D. Miller, *Capitalism: An Ethnographic Approach* (Oxford: Berg, 1997). For this section, see also D. Miller, ed., *Car Cultures* (Oxford: Berg, 2001).

8 See S. Vertovec, *Hindu Trinidad* (London: Macmillan, 1992).

9 Some of the same material has already been given in *Stuff* (pp. 99–106), though on this occasion I am making several different points.

10 *The Bomb*, 21 December 1990.

11 There is more extensive evidence to support this conclusion in the more detailed analysis of the house that appears within Miller, *Modernity: An Ethnographic Approach*, pp. 206–19.

12 Some of these arguments go back to Miller, *Material Culture and Mass Consumption*.

13 J. Baudrillard, *For a Critique of the Political Economy of the Sign* (St Louis, MO: Telos Press, 1981).

14 S. Drakulić, *How We Survived Communism and Even Laughed* (London: Hutchinson, 1992).

15 Baudrillard, *For a Critique of the Political Economy of the Sign*.

16 This section is mainly from D. Miller, 'Christmas against materialism in Trinidad', but also from D. Miller, 'A theory of Christmas', both in D. Miller, ed., *Unwrapping Christmas* (Oxford: Oxford University Press, 1993), pp. 3–37, 134–53.

17 Trinidad's *Sunday Guardian* magazine, 16 December 1990.

18 R. Belk, 'Materialism and the making of the modern American Christmas', in Miller, ed., *Unwrapping Christmas*, pp. 75–104.

Chapter 3 Why We Shop

1 Much of this section is taken from D. Miller, *The Dialectics of Shopping* (Chicago: University of Chicago Press, 2001), especially pp. 17–56.

2 Typically, P. Underhill, *Why We Buy: The Science of Shopping* (New York: Simon & Schuster, 1999).

3 Now a professor of design history in Vienna, with many publications of her own from this and other projects.

4 When I say a random street, I usually select one simply because it is a convenient place for both me and my collaborator to reach. But there is some selection going on. We are avoiding streets which as a whole look either conspicuously wealthy or impoverished. In this study of shopping we picked a street that had large family houses at one end and what was then a council estate at the other, and so seemed likely to yield a range of incomes.

5 D. Miller, 'How infants grow mothers in North London', *Theory, Culture and Society*, 14/4 (1997): 67–88.

6 B. Simpson, 'On gifts, payments and disputes: divorce and changing family structures in contemporary Britain', *Journal of the Royal Anthropological Institute*, 3 (1997): 731–45.

7 Much of this section comes from D. Miller, *A Theory of Shopping* (Cambridge: Polity, 1998).

8 L. Layne, ed., *Transformative Motherhood* (New York: Routledge, 1999); and Layne, 'He was a real baby with baby things: a material culture analysis of personhood, parenthood and pregnancy loss', *Journal of Material Culture*, 5 (2000): 321–45. See also D. Miller, *Stuff* (Cambridge: Polity, 2010), p. 136.

9 Discussed also in the book *Stuff*. But I assume some readers may not have read that work.

10 D. Miller, *The Dialectics of Shopping* (Chicago: University of Chicago Press, 2001), pp. 42–4.

11 P. Bourdieu, *Distinction: A Social Critique of the Judgement of Taste* (London: Routledge & Kegan Paul, 1979).

12 This section comes from D. Miller, P. Jackson, N. Thift, N. B. Holbrook and M. Rowlands, *Shopping, Place, and Identity* (London: Routledge, 1998).

13 This section comes from Miller, *A Theory of Shopping*.

14 H. Hubert and M. Mauss, *Sacrifice: Its Nature and Function* (Chicago: University of Chicago Press, 1964). Other important discussions in anthropology include L. de Heusch, *Sacrifice in Africa* (Manchester: Manchester University Press, 1985); M. Detienne and J.-P. Vernant, eds, *The Cuisine of Sacrifice among the Greeks* (Chicago: University of Chicago Press, 1989); and V. Valeri, *Kingship and Sacrifice* (Chicago: University of Chicago Press, 1985).

15 See, especially, S. Gudeman and A. Rivera, *Conversations in Colombia* (Cambridge: Cambridge University Press, 1990).

16 Much of this section is taken from Miller, *The Dialectics of Shopping*, especially pp. 120–44.

17 N. Gregson, L. Crewe and K. Brooks, 'Shopping space and practice', *Environment and Planning D: Society and Space*, 20 (2002): 597–617.

Chapter 4   Why Denim?

1 The material for this chapter is taken from several publications, including D. Miller and S. Woodward, 'A manifesto for the study of denim', *Social Anthropology*, 15/3 (2007): 335–51; D. Miller and S. Woodward, eds, *Global Denim* (Oxford: Berg, 2011); S. Woodward and D. Miller, 'Unravelling denim', *Textile*, 9/1 (2011): 7–10; and D. Miller and S. Woodward, *Blue Jeans: The Art of Ordinary* (Berkeley: University of California Press, 2012).

2 This was really the point of D. Miller, ed., *Acknowledging Consumption* (London: Routledge, 1995).

3 D. Miller, *Material Culture and Mass Consumption* (Oxford: Blackwell, 1987), pp. 85–108.

4 Various statistics of jeans purchasing, in the UK and worldwide, are given in the introduction to Miller and Woodward, eds, *Global Denim*.

5 D. Miller, 'The little black dress is the solution – but what's the problem?', in K. Ekstrom and H. Brembeck, eds, *Elusive Consumption* (Oxford: Berg, 2004), pp. 113–27.

6 S. Woodward, *Why Women Wear What they Wear* (Oxford: Berg, 2007).

7 The following section is taken from D. Miller, 'Buying time', in E. Shove, F. Trentmann and R. Wilk, eds, *Time, Consumption and Everyday Life* (Oxford: Berg, 2009), pp. 157–70.

8 M. Akgun et al., 'Silicosis caused by sandblasting of jeans in Turkey: a report of two concomitant cases', *Journal of Occupational Health*, 47 (2005): 346–9; A. Cimrin et al., 'Sandblasting jeans kills young people', *European Respiratory Journal*, 28/4 (2006): 885–6.

9 I once wore a pair of Diesels intermittently for two years before washing them, without anyone complaining that I smelt or dogs becoming particularly affectionate. It was worth it for the exclamations of horror from my students when I mentioned this in a lecture.

10 www.ucl.ac.uk/global-denim-project/.

11 I have pretty much never been successful at applying for funding for my research, but for my proposal on denim the Arts and Humanities Council gave me the lowest rating they have in their rulebook, below anything I had previously known existed. So the fact that I came to feel that this largely unfunded research ended up

as one of my most successful programmes was not altogether displeasing.

12 All these papers are to be found in either Miller and Woodward, eds, *Global Denim*, or Woodward and Miller, 'Unravelling denim'.

13 S. Comstock, 'The making of an American icon: the transformation of blue jeans during the Great Depression', in Miller and Woodward, eds, *Global Denim*, pp. 23–50.

14 Perhaps the best basic history is J. Sullivan, *Jeans: A Cultural History of an American Icon* (New York: Gotham Press, 2006).

15 J. Balfour-Paul, *Indigo* (London: British Museum Press, 1998).

16 M. Taussig, 'Redeeming indigo', *Theory, Culture and Society*, 25/3 (2008): 1–15.

17 D. Miller, 'The limits of jeans in Kannu', in Miller and Woodward, eds, *Global Denim*, pp. 87–101.

18 The main publication of the London ethnography is Miller and Woodward, *Blue Jeans: The Art of Ordinary*.

19 For example, R. Barthes, *The Fashion System* (London: Cape, 1967); M. Sahlins, *Culture and Practical Reason* (Chicago: University of Chicago Press, 1976).

20 Strictly speaking, nothing can be post-semiotic, since at the least it would then symbolise the state of being non-symbolic. I also have to acknowledge a further contradiction. To the degree that I now go on to suggest that jeans specifically signify the state of ordinary, they cannot be post-semiotic, because ordinary is a particular state. Although I am then logically incorrect, I would justify my use of the term post-semiotic since I have found it to be a very effective way of making the larger points about the importance and consequence of wearing jeans today, which is the larger aim of this research project.

21 R. Johnston, J. Forrest and M. Poulsen, 'Are there ethnic enclaves/ghettos in English cities?', *Urban Studies*, 39 (2002): 591–618; C. Peach, 'Does Britain have ghettos?', *Transactions of the Institute of British Geographers*, 21 (1996): 216–35; and L. Simpson, 'Ghettos of the mind: the empirical behaviour of indices of segregation and diversity', *Journal of the Royal Statistical Society: Series A*, 170 (2007): 405–24.

22 D. Miller, *The Comfort of Things* (Cambridge: Polity, 2008), pp. 179–85.

23 For the trade in second-hand clothes with areas such as Africa and India, see K. Hansen, *Salaula: The World of Secondhand Clothing and Zambia* (Chicago: University of Chicago Press, 2000); and L. Norris, *Recycling Indian Clothing* (Bloomington: University of Indiana Press, 2010).

24 Which is another reason why, as noted many times in this book, we should not try and study society using hypotheses and tests.
25 Miller and Woodward, *Blue Jeans: The Art of Ordinary*. See also D. Miller, 'Anthropology in blue jeans', *American Ethnologist*, 37/3 (2010): 415–28.
26 Ibid.

Chapter 5   It's the Stupid Economy

1 J. Baudriallard, *For a Critique of the Political Economy of the Sign* (St Louis, MO: Telos Press, 1981).
2 N. McKenrick, J. Brewer and J. H. Plumb, *The Birth of a Consumer Society* (London: Hutchinson, 1983).
3 D. Miller, *Material Culture and Mass Consumption* (Oxford: Blackwell, 1987).
4 Much of the following section is taken from D. Miller, *Capitalism: An Ethnographic Approach* (Oxford: Berg, 1997).
5 Ibid.
6 A television series, produced by Lionsgate, portraying the US advertising industry of the 1950s and 1960s and starring some of the finest lingerie of the period.
7 For the problematic impact of structural adjustment in the Caribbean, see K. McAfee, *Storm Signals: Structural Adjustment and Development Alternatives in the Caribbean* (London: Zed Books, 1991).
8 H.-J. Chang, *23 Things They Don't Tell You about Capitalism* (London: Allen Lane, 2010), pp. 74–87.
9 K. Ho, *Liquidated: An Ethnography of Wall Street* (Durham, NC: Duke University Press, 2009), p. 209. Other examples of ethnographic studies of finance include D. Stark, *The Sense of Dissonance* (Princeton, NJ: Princeton University Press, 2009), pp. 118–62); and C. Zaloom, *Out of the Pits: Traders and Technology from Chicago to London* (Chicago: University of Chicago Press, 2006).
10 A. Ouroussoff, *Wall Street at War: The Secret Struggle for the Global Economy* (Cambridge: Polity, 2010).
11 G. Bickerstaffe, ed., *Mastering Finance* (London: Pitman, 1998). The book is actually an edited series of essays, but for my purposes I am treating it as a whole.
12 Ibid., p. 6.
13 Ibid., p. 19.
14 H. Miyazaki, 'The materiality of finance theory', in D. Miller, ed., *Materiality* (Durham, NC: Duke University Press, 2005), pp. 165–81.

15   Ibid., p. 32.
16   Ibid., p. 9.
17   Ibid., pp. 167–8.
18   Ibid., p. 169.
19   Ibid., pp. 43–8.
20   Ibid., p. 47.
21   An example of the kind of books on epistemology we were reading at the time would be R. Bhaskar, *The Possibility of Naturalism* (Brighton: Harvester, 1979).
22   B. Latour, *We Have Never Been Modern* (Hemel Hempstead: Harvester Wheatsheaf, 1993).
23   See T. Bayliss-Smith and S. Wanmali, *Understanding Green Revolutions* (Cambridge: Cambridge University Press, 1984).
24   It is, however, accepted practice to return for short studies to places where a full ethnography has already been carried out – as, in my case, with repeated research projects based in Trinidad.
25   D. McCloskey, *The Rhetoric of Economics* (2nd edn, Madison: University of Wisconsin Press, 1998).
26   For example, E. Fullbrook, ed., *Real World Economics: A Post-Autistic Economics Reader* (London: Anthem Press, 2007), and a journal, *The Real World Economics Review*.
27   Some of this section follows D. Miller, 'The unintended political economy', in P. du Gay and M. Pryke, eds, *Cultural Economy: Cultural Analysis and Commercial Life* (London: Sage, 2002), pp. 166–84.
28   D. Henwood, *Wall Street* (London: Verso, 1998).
29   Ibid., p. 72.
30   Ibid., p. 3.
31   Ibid., p. 76; see also p. 155.
32   Ibid., p. 3.
33   Ibid., p. 187.
34   J. M. Keynes, *The Collected Writings of John Maynard Keynes*, vol. VII, p. 159, cited ibid., pp. 206–7.
35   B. Burrough and J. Helyar, *Barbarians at the Gate* (London: Arrow Books, 1990).
36   M. Lewis, *Liar's Poker* (London: Hodder & Stoughton, 1989).
37   M. Lewis, *The Big Short* (London: Penguin, 2010).
38   Ibid., p. 105.
39   Ibid., p. 72.
40   Ibid., p. 225.
41   G. Clark, *Pension Fund Capitalism* (Oxford: Oxford University Press, 2000). Clark has maintained an admirable concern for the subsequent regulation and governance of pension funds. See

G. Clark and R. Unwin, 'Innovative models of pension fund govern-ance in the context of the global financial crisis', *Pensions*, 15/1 (2010): 62–7.

42   P. Drucker, 'Reckoning with the pension fund revolution', *Harvard Business Review* (1991), March–April: 106–14.

43   Clark, *Pension Fund Capitalism*, p. 272.

44   See N. Thrift, 'The rise of soft capitalism', *Cultural Values*, 1 (1997): 29–57.

45   J. O'Shea and C. Madigan, *Dangerous Company: The Consulting Powerhouses and the Businesses they Save and Ruin* (London: Nicholas Brealey, 1997). Another example is D. Craig, *Rip-off!: The Scandalous Inside Story of the Management Consulting Money Machine* (published by the author, 2005).

46   For a typical textbook, see A. Rappaport, *Creating Shareholder Value: The New Standard for Business Performance* (New York: Free Press, 1986). For a helpful general discussion, see J. Froud, C. Haslam, S. Johal and K. Williams, 'Shareholder value and the political economy of late capitalism', *Economy and Society*, 29/1 (2000): 1–12.

47   T. Copeland, T. Koller and J. Murrin, *Valuation: Measuring and Managing the Value of Companies* (2nd edn, New York: John Wiley, 1994).

48   Ibid., p. 3.

49   Ibid., p. 31.

50   K. Ho, *Liquidated: An Ethnography of Wall Street* (Durham, NC: Duke University Press, 2009).

51   Ibid., p. 127.

52   Ibid., p. 157.

53   For this trend to short termism, see, as well as Ho, W. Hutton, *The State We're In* (London: Jonathan Cape, 1995).

54   McCloskey, *The Rhetoric of Economics*.

55   Chang, *23 Things They Don't Tell You about Capitalism*, pp. 17–22.

56   H. Davies, *The Financial Crisis: Who Is to Blame?* (Cambridge: Polity, 2010).

57   Ibid., pp. 177–84.

58   www2.lse.ac.uk/fmg/researchProgrammes/paulWoolleyCentre/home.

59   The belief that, notwithstanding its many evils, the economists' world is the best of all possible worlds.

60   For example, A. Sen, 'Rational fools: a critique of the behavioural foundations of economic theory', *Philosophy and Public Affairs*, 6/4 (1977): 317–44.

61 I have discussed this most fully in D. Miller, *The Dialectics of Shopping* (Chicago: University of Chicago Press, 2001), pp. 176–205.

62 Much of this section comes from D. Miller, 'The virtual moment', *Journal of the Royal Anthropological Institute*, 9 (2003): 57–75.

63 It is symptomatic of the impact of audit that one no longer knows or cares what these letters stand for; it seems more significant that we are now answerable mainly to acronyms.

64 Mine was one of several works on audit by anthropologists. See M. Strathern, ed., *Audit Cultures: Anthropological Studies in Accountability, Ethics and the Academy* (London: Routledge, 2000). See also M. Power, *The Audit Society: Rituals of Verification* (Oxford: Oxford University Press, 1997).

65 See S. Martin, 'Implementing Best Value: local public services in transition', *Public Administration*, 78/1 (2000): 209–27.

66 M. Weber, 'Politics as a vocation', in *From Max Weber*, ed. H.H. Gerth and C. Wright Mills (London: Routledge & Kegan Paul, 1948).

67 Taken at the time of study from www.idea.gov.uk – but I did not record the exact date – sorry.

68 Much of this section comes from D. Miller, 'A theory of virtualism', in J. Carrier and D. Miller, eds, *Virtualism: A New Political Economy* (Oxford: Berg, 1998), pp. 187–215.

69 For some more general discussion of the implications of consumer authority, see R. Keat, N. Whiteley and N. Abercrombie, eds, *The Authority of the Consumer* (London: Routledge, 1994), pp. 189–206.

70 I actually regret the term, because several publications that have cited my work on a theory of virtualism have confused the two and assume I mean virtual in the digital sense, but hopefully this will help separate them out again.

71 Particularly helpful is MacKenzie's book on how the material manifestations of these calculative practices actually make markets, of which the one very deliberate example is the recent manufacture of a market in carbon. See D. MacKenzie, *Material Markets: How Economic Agents are Constructed* (Oxford: Oxford University Press, 2009). See also M. Callon, ed., *The Laws of the Market* (Oxford: Blackwell, 1998).

72 N. Thrift, *Knowing Capitalism* (London: Sage, 2005).

73 Much of this section comes from D. Miller, 'The uses of value', *Geoforum*, 39 (2008): 1122–32.

74 K. Marx, *Capital*, Vol. 1 (London: Lawrence & Wishart, 1970), p. 97.

75 For an interesting parallel argument set more within business, see D. Stark, *The Sense of Dissonance* (Princeton, NJ: Princeton University Press, 2009).

76 V. Zelizer, *Pricing the Priceless Child* (New York: Basic Books, 1985).

77 V. Zelizer, *The Purchase of Intimacy* (Princeton, NJ: Princeton University Press, 2005).

78 For example, a survey by the Consumer Association journal *Which?* placed John Lewis as best high-street retailer for 2009.

79 For analyses of the John Lewis Partnership, see, for its industrial relations, A. Flanders, R. Pomeranz and J. Woodward, *Experiments in Industrial Democracy* (London: Faber, 1968), and, for the business performance side of things, K. Bradley and S. Taylor, *Business Performance in the Retail Sector* (Oxford: Clarendon Press, 1992).

80 M. Rojas, *The Rise and Fall of the Swedish Model* (London: Social Market Foundation, 1998).

81 These both come from wealthy economies. When it comes to many states then, to invert Marx, I still feel the socialist-inflected assault on inequality may be the necessary precursor towards social democratic capitalism, a transition embodied perhaps by Lula for Brazil and the earlier communist government in Kerala.

82 The analogy with anthropology as a whole is perhaps clearest when anthropologists try and write textbooks on economic anthropology. Ever since the original tussle between what were called formalists, who emphasised economic rationality, and substantivists, who emphasised cultural context, these have inevitably been attempts to reconcile economics with a moral and social concern for people. My favourite example is R. Wilk, *Economics and Culture* (Boulder, CO: Westview Press, 1996), but see also K. Hart, *The Memory Bank* (London: Profile, 2000), and C. Hann and K. Hart, *Economic Anthropology* (Cambridge: Polity, 2011).

Chapter 6   How Not to Save a Planet

1 Mike's arguments can be found in much more detail in D. Miller, 'Could the internet de-fetishise the commodity?', *Environment and Planning D: Society and Space*, 21/3 (2003): 359–72. See also S. O'Neill and M. Boykoff, 'The role of new media in engaging the public with climate', in L. Whitmarsh, S. O'Neill and I. Lorenzoni, eds, *Engaging the Public with Climate Change* (London: Earthscan, 2011), pp. 233–51.

2   D. Miller, 'Buying time', in E. Shove, F. Trentmann and R. Wilk, eds, *Time, Consumption and Everyday Life* (Oxford: Berg, 2009), pp. 157–70.

3   For the issues of waste, see chapter 4, note 23, and other studies that were associated with the 'Waste of the World' project led by Nicky Gregson. See also G. Hawkins, *The Ethics of Waste* (Lanham, MD: Rowman & Littlefield, 2006).

4   Tom is of course my PhD student. It was not just that this was an excellent fieldsite, but Tom is an outstanding ethnographic field-worker, who, with fluent language skills, seemed to be everyone's best friend and was able to show me in astonishing detail the private and public face of everyday town life in China.

5   A. Mol, 'Environmental reform in modernizing China', in M. Red-clift and G. Woodgate, eds, *The International Handbook of Environmental Sociology* (2nd edn, Cheltenham: Edward Elgar, 2010), pp. 378–93.

6   Most readily available is the Intergovernmental Panel on Climate Change, *Fourth Assessment Report: Climate Change 2007*, 3 vols (Cambridge: Cambridge University Press, 2007), but, for the gist of it, see www.ipcc.ch/publications_and_data/publications_ipcc_ fourth_assessment_report_synthesis_report.htm.

7   D. Meadows et al., *The Limits to Growth: A Report for the Club of Rome's Project on the Predicament of Mankind* (New York: New American Library, 1972).

8   This is quite a common theme in Monbiot's weekly column in *The Guardian*.

9   The connections down the fashion commodity chain are brought out very clearly in L. Siegle, *To Die For: Is Fashion Wearing out the World?* (London: Fourth Estate, 2011).

10 Among recent works that make these points are D. Harvey, *A Brief History of Neoliberalism* (Oxford: Oxford University Press, 2005), and D. Harvey, *The Enigma of Capital: And the Crises of Capitalism* (London: Profile, 2011).

11 T. Jackson, *Prosperity without Growth: Economics for a Finite Planet* (London: Earthscan, 2009).

12 For an extremely interesting account of this, see Donald MacKenzie, *Material Markets* (Oxford: Oxford University Press, 2009), pp. 137–76. There are actually a number of versions of the carbon market, including the Clean Development Mechanism (CDM), sanctioned by Kyoto, and UN REDD, backed by Norway among others, but they all trade or claim to mitigate rather than directly reduce usage.

13 N. Stern, *The Economics of Climate Change* (Cambridge: Cambridge University Press, 2006).
14 Ibid., pp. 368–92, 530–54.
15 Ibid., pp. 351–67.
16 Ibid., p. 399.
17 Ibid., p. 409.
18 Ibid., p. 427.
19 Ibid., pp. 49–58.
20 Ibid., p. 292. On a recent trip there I found not everyone in Iceland welcomes the suggestion.
21 *The Economist*, 30 April 2011, p. 62.
22 George Monbiot, 'Cameron's "green growth" policy looks naïve today. It will look cynical in 2027', *The Guardian*, 24 May 2011, p. 27.
23 C. Isenhour, 'Building sustainable societies: exploring sustainability policy and practice in the age of high consumption', PhD dissertation, University of Kentucky. See also C. Isenhour, 'Building sustainable societies: a Swedish case study on the limits of reflexive modernization', *American Ethnologist*, 37/3 (2010): 511–25, and C. Isenhour, 'On conflicted Swedish consumers: the effort to stop shopping and neoliberal environmental governance', *Journal of Consumer Behaviour*, 9/6 (2010): 454–69.
24 Isenhour, 'Building sustainable societies: exploring sustainability policy and practice in the age of high consumption', p. 20.
25 K. Norgaard, *Living in Denial: Climate Change, Emotions, and Everyday Life* (Cambridge, MA: MIT Press, 2011).
26 F. DeBrabander, 'The Green Revolution backfires: Sweden's lesson for real sustainability', 10 June 2011, www.commondreams.org/view/2011/06/10-3.
27 G. Monbiot, *Heat* (London: Allen Lane, 2006).
28 Greenwashing is discussed in several of the papers in T. Lewis and E. Potter, eds, *Ethical Consumption* (London: Routledge, 2011) – for example, J. Littler, 'What's so wrong with ethical consumption?', pp. 27–39.
29 For economists finding ways of not ceding authority to consumers but only appearing to do so, see D. Miller, 'A theory of virtualism', in J. Carrier and D. Miller, eds, *Virtualism: A New Political Economy* (Oxford: Berg, 1998), pp. 187–215.
30 A. Giddens, *The Politics of Climate Change* (Cambridge: Polity, 2010).
31 A. Sen, 'Capability and well-being', in M. Nussbaum and A. Sen, eds, *The Quality of Life* (Oxford: Clarendon Press, 1993), pp. 30–53.

32 H. Wilhite, *Consumption and the Transformation of Everyday Life: A View from South India* (London: Palgrave Macmillan, 2008).

33 There are many such scenarios in H. Girardet and M. Mendonca, *A Renewable World* (London: Green Books, 2009).

34 R. Baron, D. Montgomery and S. Tuladhar, 'Black carbon migration', in B. Lomborg, ed., *Smart Solutions to Climate Change* (Cambridge: Cambridge University Press, 2010), pp. 142–58.

35 B. Bilger, 'Hearth surgery', *New Yorker*, 21 December 2009, repr. in J. Dibbell, ed., *The Best Technology Writing 2010* (New Haven, CT: Yale University Press, 2011), pp. 137–64.

36 My other reason for not discussing the idea of digital sustainability here is that it is something I hope to write more about elsewhere.

37 The popular version that students enjoyed debating in those days came from A. J. Ayer, *Language, Truth and Logic* (London: Gollancz, 1936).

38 See, for example, B. Latour, *Pandora's Box* (Cambridge, MA: Harvard University Press, 1999).

39 D. Victor, *Climate Change: Debating America's Policy Options* (New York: Council on Foreign Relations, 2004), p. 11.

40 R. Pielke, *The Climate Fix* (New York: Basic Books, 2010), pp. 1–34.

41 According to M. Berners-Lee, *How Bad are Bananas? The Carbon Footprint of Everything* (London: Profile Books, 2010), p. 17, the paper towel has a CO_2 footprint of 10 gm, while that of the dryer is 20 gm.

42 Ibid., p. 135.

43 The study of the webcam and its impact, including the idea that this could be part of a wider programme of digital sustainability, is in fact my current research project.

44 P. Ghemawat, *World 3.0: World Prosperity and How to Achieve it* (Boston: Harvard Business Review Press, 2011), p. 116.

45 An exemplary book that helped stimulate further research was E. Shove, *Comfort, Cleanliness and Convenience* (Oxford: Berg, 2003). For an earlier anthropological study, see R. Wilk and H. Wilhite, 'Why don't people weatherize their homes? An ethnographic solution', *Energy*, 10/5 (1985), pp. 621–9.

46 A typical example of this green liberalism would be R. Paehkle and D. Torgerson, 'Environmental politics and the administrative state', in R. Paehkle and D. Torgerson, eds, *Managing Leviathan* (Peterborough, Ontario: Broadview Press, 2005), pp. 313–26.

47 Books on the politics of climate change include Giddens, *The Politics of Climate Change*, and M. Howes, *Politics and the*

Environment: Risk and the Role of Government and Industry (Crows Nest, NSW: Allen & Unwin, 2005).

48 Pielke, *The Climate Fix*, pp. 191–216.
49 ICANN = the Internet Corporation for Assigned Names and Numbers.
50 The World Intellectual Property Organisation (WIPO) was formed by the United Nations in 1970.
51 Thanks to Rick Wilk for these points.
52 See, for example, G. Hosein, 'Food, family, art and God: aesthetics authority in public life in Trinidad', in D. Miller, ed., *Anthropology and the Individual* (Oxford: Berg, 2009), pp. 159–77.
53 A. Sen, *The Idea of Justice* (London: Allen Lane, 2009).
54 W. Hutton, *Them and Us* (London: Little, Brown, 2010).
55 BRIC stands for Brazil, Russia, India and China.
56 Ghemawat, *World 3.0.*, pp. 25–9, and Giddens, *The Politics of Climate Change*, pp. 207–12.
57 The discount card for members of the Campaign for Real Ale is of considerable benefit to those of us who are fond of good quality British beer. I figured I ought to end this book with at least one practical pointer in the direction of improved consumption.

Index